Also by Harold L. Lustig

4 Steps to Financial Security for
Lesbian and Gay Couples

Naked in the Nursing Home
www.nakedinthenursinghome.com
www.haroldlustig.com

Published by:
Blooming Twig Books
PO Box 4668 #66675
New York, NY 10163-4668
www.bloomingtwig.com

ISBN 978-1-933918-64-8

First Edition, First Printing

When you land in a nursing home, you are stripped of your privacy, privilege, and power. You are naked and defenseless.

NAKED IN THE NURSING HOME

The Women's Guide to Paying for Long-Term Care Without Going Broke

By

Harold L. Lustig

Blooming Twig Books
New York / 2011

To
my wife Rindy,
an RN who understands

NAKED IN THE
NURSING HOME

The Women's Guide to Paying for
Long-Term Care Without Going Broke

By

Harold L. Lustig

Foreword by Rick Law, Esq

ACKNOWLEDGMENTS

The challenge in writing a book on long-term care planning is gaining an understanding of Medicaid and VA benefits. My thanks go to David J. Zumpano, CPA and attorney, who provided legal review and comments for the technical issues in Medicaid and VA benefits as well as the attorney's section of Chapter One.

While research is fine, talking directly to the authority is even better. I want to thank Rabbi Bennett Blum, MD, for his help and work in protecting elders from financial abuse.

Bob Scrivano, a long-term care planning consultant for his quick response in reviewing chapters.

Rick Law, Esq. for his insightful comments and fabulous Foreword.

Jo Huey, The Alzheimer's Advocate®, Founder and President of the Alzheimer's Caregiver Institute, who helped set the stage for my understanding of what Alzheimer's disease is really all about.

Larry Moore, Director of Marketing at American Independent Marketing, who reviewed the Long-Term Care chapter and made sure I got it right.

Tom Orr, President of Senior Insurance Training Services, whose LTCi mentoring and teaching has proven most helpful over the years.

Candice Moses, Director of Marketing at Aegis Living of Moraga who reviewed the "What is Long-Term Care" chapter.

Kent Gustavson, who transformed the manuscript into an exciting book, empowered me to come up with the title, and educated me on the nuances of the publishing business.

And my wife, Clarinda Cole Lustig, who didn't mind my disappearing at 5 a.m. and the evening hours to write this book and whose support enabled me to keep going.

Table of Contents

FOREWORD

No one wants to be out of money or out of options before they're out of breath. If you are either a Boomer or one of the Greatest Generation, then this book may save your health and your wealth. Harold Lustig has filled this book with difficult-to-find information that will help you to protect your assets, find the most appropriate insurance for your needs, learn about wartime veteran long-term care benefits, and protect valuable government benefits for nursing home care.

Harold has dedicated his life to counseling people just like you about financial investments, estate planning, and successful aging. He knows both the most frequently asked questions and the unknown questions that should be asked. That's right—this book is packed with answers to the questions that should be asked—but most people would never think to ask. This easy-to-understand book was written to provide you with a road map to keep you on track and out of the ditch.

I am a Chicago-based elder law attorney who serves seniors and those who love them. Elder law attorneys serve the frail, the elderly, and their families. We know that most often the burden of long-term care falls upon the wives and the daughters. After all, women have a much longer life expectancy than men. Wives and daughters most often wind up making health care decisions for their aging loved ones. Long-term care is a woman's nightmare. You can prevent that nightmare from happening to you and your family if you read and act on what Harold shares with you in this book.

Recently there have been many drastic changes involving Medicare, ObamaCare, and nursing home benefits. These changes are so revolutionary that your estate and financial plan needs to be revisited. Your old estate and financial plan are based on old information and ideas which are now totally antiquated. Harold provides up-to-the-minute recommendations which can save you tens of thousands of dollars. If you have to walk through a minefield, the best way to do it is to follow somebody. Investing for prosperity in retirement is like a minefield. Harold is a trustworthy guide who knows the way.

This book is designed to provide you with easy-to-understand action steps to help you:

1. Protect yourself from elder financial abuse;

2. Find an honest and capable elder law attor ney;

3. Preserve your eligibility for valuable governmental benefits to pay for nursing home care;

4. Understand Veterans Administration benefits to pay for in-home and nursing facility costs.

I highly recommend that you take this book to the cashier—so that you will not be out of money and out of options before you're out of breath.

Rick L. Law[1]
Law Elder Law, LLP

---

1 Rick Law, Esq. Aurora, IL *www.lawelderlaw.com*, 630-585-5200.

PREFACE

My father, at 78, came to me and said he had outlived his assets. I was living in San Francisco. My brother was in Chicago raising three children and my parents were in Baltimore. My brother and I were completely surprised. Whenever we spoke to our parents, they said things were fine. I did not know what to do. That event changed my professional life and I focused my financial planning efforts on retirement and estate planning.

Six years later, Stephanie, my mother, became chronically ill. My parents did not know what help was available; like so many families, they were lost. Already out of assets, living on Social Security and a miniscule pension, they struggled with Medicare, the hospital, and the nursing facility for help and continuing care. Had I known then what I know now, my parents would have qualified for Medicaid and other financial help; their quality of life in the end would have been significantly better.

Like many families, my brother and I did not see our parents' needs coming. I wrote this book and do the work I do because I do not want you, your parents, or your loved ones to go through what my family endured.

I wrote my first book, *4 Steps to Financial Security for Lesbian and Gay Couples* to help a community that wasn't being served. In many ways women have the same problem; they are not adequately served, and hence, are not prepared. As Rick Law said in the Foreword, long-term care is a woman's nightmare. Families wouldn't go broke or be destroyed if they were prepared.

I wrote this book to empower you to prepare. Smokey the Bear was right; it's in your hands. Enjoy the book; it's been a wonderful journey writing it for you. Please e-mail me with your experiences, feelings, and stories to Harold@HaroldLustig.com

Harold L. Lustig CLU, ChFC
Estate and Elder Planning Associates
San Rafael, CA

MYTHS

◎ My kids will take care of me.

◎ Medicare pays for long-term care.

◎ My spouse will be fine if I need care.

◎ It won't happen to me.

◎ I'll never qualify for long-term care insurance.

◎ Long-term care insurance is too expensive.

◎ I have to give my assets away to get the government to pay for my care.

◎ There are no tax benefits with long-term care insurance.

◎ I'll lose my house to get government help.

◎ I am not entitled to a Veterans Pension to help pay for my care.

◎ My children will go broke paying for my care.

◎ Mom and Dad are in fine financial shape.

◎ I'm in my forties; I don't need long-term care protection.

Let's dispel these myths!

IS THIS GUIDE FOR YOU?

This guide is designed to help women plan for long-term care. While modern medicine has ensured that we live longer and our bodies remain strong, it has not ensured that our minds remain strong. The tremendous expansion of need for care at home and in long-term care facilities has grown exponentially due to our aging brain and what we call dementia and Alzheimer's. While our bodies are being maintained, the loss of mental capacity has created a whole new epidemic to Americans and the financial system.[2]

There are two groups of individuals that this guide can help—those who are in crisis and those who have time to plan ahead. If you or a loved one has one foot in the nursing home or has been diagnosed with Alzheimer's disease, Parkinson's disease, or any chronic condition and is not prepared, you are in crisis or will be very soon. If your loved one is in a hospital or a nursing home and you have little or no information on what is going on with them medically or financially, you are in crisis or will be very soon. This guide will help you.

If you and your loved ones are healthy, it's time to plan ahead NOW. You cannot wait until a health problem arises. Avoiding a crisis maximizes your options. This guide will help you identify what you need to know and how to get peace of mind.

Some basic facts to keep in mind:

⊚ The odds of needing care are high—greater than one in two at age 65,

---

2 In his book, *The Myth of Alzheimer's*, Peter J. Whitehead, M.D., Ph.D., says "In our modern age, in which remarkable scientific and technological advances have both extended and brought quality of human lives, we find major challenges to our rationality and values as science attempts to understand our own mysterious organ of rational thought—the brain—and the very process of brain aging. From out of the depths of this paradox, a hundred year old monster has risen; it is called 'Alzheimer's disease.' 2007, p. 3.

much higher than other risks we routinely insure like automobiles and houses.[3]

◎ Long-term care happens to people of all ages (over 40 percent of people who need care are under age 65).[4]

◎ Health insurance and Medicare do not pay for long-term care.

There are numerous insurance plans, Medicaid strategies, VA benefits, and legal documents that may protect you when you can no longer take care of yourself or a loved one. New federal and state laws dramatically affect long-term care and asset protection planning!

If you can afford to spend between $51,000 to $116,000[5] or more per year depending on where you or a loved one receives nursing care for an extended disability, then parts of this book can be skipped. Home care can be more expensive. If, on the other hand, you had not planned for one of life's three D's (divorce, disease, or death) and are faced with a long-term care need for yourself or a loved one, you may find yourself in crisis.

If you have questions about who can make decisions when you cannot decide about the levels of care, this guide is for you. If you are concerned about your ability to stay at home when you or a loved one has a major chronic illness requiring caregiving, this guide is for you. If you do not know if you will be able to keep your family together and maintain your lifestyle, or if you do not know how to protect your assets or maximize your options, then this guide is a must-read.

---

3 Shelton, Phyllis. Worksite Long-Term Care Insurance Toolbox. 2010. p. 56.
4 Ibid.
5 Per Genworth 2010 Cost of Care Survey. Costs vary by state and where you live. The average room rate in Louisiana was $51,000, while in NY state, the average rate was $116,000. Semi–private rates are less.

WHY WOMEN?

The last person standing will most likely be a woman! We've all been told that women outlive men and that women are the caregivers. As important as that is, the reasons for understanding the risks you face are deeper, more complex, and more compelling for using the information in this guide. American women are losing their dreams every day because a parent, a loved one, or spouse has a severe stroke, accident, MS, Parkinson's, Alzheimer's disease, or any of the myriad other conditions that require caregiving. You must protect yourself.

Women are the caregivers—both paid and unpaid. The paid help (home health aides and nursing home aides) are among the most oppressed part of the US job market. They are asked to take care of an increasingly frail population for minimum wage at great risk of physical injury to themselves. These brave women perform heavy labor every day by lifting, turning, and cleaning sometimes heavy and immobile patients.[6]

The unpaid caregivers are women, usually daughters, daughters-in-law, and spouses. These silent caregivers are asked to be the primary caregivers in addition to full- or part-time employment and/or raising a family.[7] The US Department of Labor says that on average, caregivers provide 18 hours of long-term care a week, but one-fifth provide 40 hours of care per week.[8]

Understanding your role in caregiving and how it can affect your life was clearly spelled out by the American Association for Long-Term Care Insurance in The 2009 Sourcebook for Long-Term Care Insurance Information.

---

6 Phyllis Shelton. *The Caregiver's Glass Ceiling,* p. 1.
7 Ibid.
8 Ibid.

You face more risks of needing care because:

◎ Women represent a greater portion of older Americans, accounting for almost 58 percent of the population over 65.

◎ Women who reach age 65 have a longer life expectancy than men.

◎ Women have 10 times the chance of reaching age 85 than men; more than two-thirds of the 85-and-older population are women.

◎ Women over age 65 are less likely to be married than men.

◎ Woman over 65 are more likely to be living alone than men.

◎ Women are far more likely to go to a nursing home.

◎ Women over 65 include 980,000 nursing home residents versus 337,000 men.

◎ Women are more likely to suffer from Alzheimer's disease.

◎ Women are more likely to suffer a stroke than men.[9]

You are typically the caregivers:

◎ Women provide between 60 to 75 percent of family or informal (non-agency) care and they spend as much as 50 percent more time providing care than men.

◎ Women do not abandon their caregiving responsibilities because of employment. As a result, women pass up promotions, job opportunities, retirement, and Social Security contributions if they are not working.

◎ Women lose Social Security benefits.

◎ Women who provide care for an ill or disabled spouse are almost six times as likely to suffer from depression as those who have no caregiving responsibilities.

◎ Women who spend nine or more hours a week caring for an ill or disabled spouse increase their risk of coronary heart disease twofold.[10]

---

9 List from the American Association for Long-term Care Insurance in *The 2009 Sourcebook for Long-term Care Insurance Information*.
10 Ibid.

CHAPTER ONE

WHAT IS LONG-TERM CARE?

"The quality of decision is like the well-timed swoop of the falcon which enables it to strike and destroy its victim."

-Sun Tzu

How long will you live? How will you live toward your end? Will you be healthy and vigorous, or frail and failing? Will you maintain your quality of life?

At the turn of the 20th century, the average life expectancy was about 47 years. Today, in the United States, the average life span is in the low 80s for women and the mid-70s for men.[11] The greatest financial threat to your retirement and peace of mind may not be the ups and downs of the stock market, but the economic consequences of you or a loved one living too long. Long-term care can be a woman's worst nightmare.

In this chapter we are going to address:

What is long-term care?
Who pays?
Who decides?
How to avoid family crisis

But first, the bad news. You have to do your homework or you will be shocked and overwhelmed when you find out what long-term care actually costs. You will be even more shocked when you learn that Medicare generally does not cover any of your costs in a nursing home or assisted living facility.[12] Disability and health insurance don't cover any of it either.

---

11 Peter J. Whitehead, M.D., Ph.D., *The Myth of Alzheimer's*, 2007, p. ix.
12 Medicare does pay minimally for some skilled nursing treatment, e.g., decubitus (bed sores) treatment and some IV therapies.

You'll be shocked to learn that it costs more for care in the home than in a facility and that it is not a do-it-yourself project. If you are the caregiver for a spouse or loved one with dementia, it can be extremely stressful and all-encompassing! There are alternatives, but first ask yourself two questions: *How will I pay for care and who will take care of me?*

At the time of this writing, the cost of long-term care was dependent on where you were getting the care and who was giving it. The median cost of long-term care in New York State, for example, was $116,000 per year for a private room and $73,000 for a semi-private room in 2010, but only $52,000 a year in Louisiana.[13] Would you send your loved one to a less expensive area? Not if you want them to survive as long as possible. People whose family, friends, and relatives visit them in a care facility live longer and maintain better health than those who have no visitors.

Planning Tip:
What is the Cost of Care?

Don't believe what it could cost? In sticker shock? You will be if you are not prepared.

Appendix A provides a sample list of the cost of care in 2010 in various cities.

Please Google "Genworth Cost of Care Survey" then pick your city or town. Or better yet, visit a few facilities near your home. The marketing director will welcome your visit.

---

13 Genworth 2010 Cost of Care Survey

WHAT IS LONG-TERM CARE?

Long-term care, also called "custodial care" or "chronic care" is provided when illness, accident, or cognitive impairment such as dementia, Alzheimer's disease, arthritis, bad knees, or other conditions affect mobility and require assistance for a person to perform the activities of daily living (ADLs).

ADLs are what you do every day. To better understand them, let's look at what you probably did this morning after you woke up. You climbed out of bed, walked to the bathroom, used the toilet, took a shower or bathed, dressed, and ate breakfast. You performed five ADLs. ADLs include bathing, eating, dressing, toileting, continence, and transferring (being able to walk and go from sitting to standing without assistance). When you need help with one ADL, generally a spouse or partner, child, or neighbor can help. Two ADLs generally require professional care from a home health care agency or assisted living facility. If you lack the ability to do three ADLs, you will require care in a nursing home.

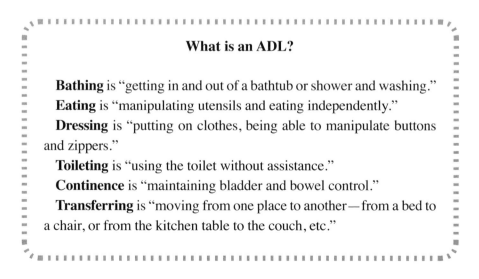

What is an ADL?

Bathing is "getting in and out of a bathtub or shower and washing."
Eating is "manipulating utensils and eating independently."
Dressing is "putting on clothes, being able to manipulate buttons and zippers."
Toileting is "using the toilet without assistance."
Continence is "maintaining bladder and bowel control."
Transferring is "moving from one place to another—from a bed to a chair, or from the kitchen table to the couch, etc."

Long-term care also refers to the continuum of care from independent living at home, assisted living, board and care, to skilled nursing care. Who pays will be determined by the type of care, who is doing it, and where the money is coming from.

1. INDEPENDENT LIVING/AT HOME CARE – At this level of care you can live at home, in a retirement community, or independently in an apartment-like setting where you can check in once a day. You, the at-home patient, can hire outside assistance, either privately or from an agency to assist with ADLs.

2. ADULT DAY CARE CENTERS – These are an alternative for families struggling with the care of an aging or disabled loved one. Adult Day Care Centers can also provide supervision and assistance on a daily basis for seniors who are not ready for assisted living or long-term care. Many even have a bus to pick up and drop off the senior.

Adult Day Care Centers have trained health care professionals. During the daytime, services are provided that allow you to continue working or to have peace of mind knowing that your loved one is cared for. While this is not a long-term care facility, these provide a respite facility to those who are providing long-term care to someone else.

3. ASSISTED LIVING – These are traditionally retirement facilities that offer additional services for a fee, such as assistance with specific ADLs. These facilities are generally for people who need some sort of help, but do not need medical care. Trained help is usually available. Assisted living facilities can be as small as for 30 people to as large as for 150 people. Help is available for laundry, housekeeping, medications, and enabling residents to live as independently as possible. Other common terms include residential care, supported care, enhanced care, personal care, and adult living facilities. Assisted living facilities permit you to maintain independence with the comfort of knowing someone is nearby to check on you or assist you with the things you struggle with.

4. **BOARD AND CARE** – Board and Care facilities are usually private homes that have been converted to care facilities and are limited to six to eight beds. You can generally drive down the block and not know that there is a Board and Care facility there.

5. **RESIDENTIAL CARE FACILITIES (RCF)** – are generally large institutions that have many residents (50 or more). Both Board and Care and RCFs offer more care than assisted living facilities. Skilled Nursing Care is not offered at this level.

6. **ALZHEIMER'S/DEMENTIA/MEMORY FACILITIES** – Many assisted living communities cater to individuals with Alzheimer's disease and other related memory disorders. There is a growing trend towards specialized communities that provide care and housing tailored to the needs of these individuals. Services can include a secure environment run by specially trained professionals skilled in handling the behavior associated with memory impairments.

7. **SKILLED NURSING FACILITIES (SNF)** – SNFs are licensed to provide Skilled Nursing Care. These facilities offer 24-hour-a-day services for those who can no longer live on their own. They have a trained staff, including nurses and sometimes doctors. Meals, housekeeping, medical, bathing, and recreation activities are all taken care of.

Planning Tip:
Choosing a Nursing Home

Do you or your loved ones think, "When I become old, I'm going to live my golden years in a nursing home?" Sometimes that decision is forced on us, many times under duress. It is a difficult and emotional decision, whether it is for us or a loved one. Selecting a nursing facility for a loved one can be a challenge. While nursing home staff can confirm vacancies, tell you how wonderful the food is, and walk you through the costs, you must ask about other charges besides room and board. (This applies to other facilities as well.) Touring the nursing home is a vital step you should take.

Here are some other questions:

1. Does the staff interact warmly with the residents and do they address them by name?

2. Can you tour other parts of the nursing home, not just the common rooms and the staged resident rooms?

3. Does the nursing home appear clean and well-maintained?

4. Are there outdoor areas for residents to enjoy?

5. Is the nursing home free of pervasive odors?

6. Do other resident rooms appear clean and well maintained?

7. What does the county ombudsperson say about this facility? Are there complaints and other issues?

8. HOSPICE – Hospice is a special care facility designed to provide a compassionate and supportive environment for individuals in the final phase of terminal illness. Hospice care enables patients to spend their last days with dignity in a comfortable environment. Hospice can be in the privacy of your home, in a hospital, in an assisted living facility, in a hospice facility, or in a nursing home. Hospice is not for long-term care or 24-hour care; it is respite care.[14]

---

14 As of this writing, hospice was a Medicare Part A covered benefit. Please call 1-800-MEDI-CARE or go to www.medicare.gov to verify.

Planning Tip:
What the Government Accounting Office Says

The Government Accounting Office (GAO) released a bulletin questioning the financial practices of continuing care communities. The GAO's concern was that the financial health of the continuing care community may not be as strong as they say. It would be a good idea to have your accountant review financial statements before you place a loved one in a facility.

Planning Tip:
How to Protect your Pocketbook

When you begin planning to protect your loved one's financial affairs or your pocketbook, it would be a good idea if you hire an RN, a Certified Case Manager, or a Certified Geriatric Care Manager to review the care practices and the charging policies for care at the facility where your loved one is.

Some facilities have been known to charge for care that they are not providing or charge for the same services multiple times. An RN would know what to look for before making a decision on a care facility or their billing practices once your loved one is admitted. You might contact your county's ombudsperson to check out their reputation. Each facility can notify you of who the ombudspersons are.

WHO PAYS?

O ne of the things that concerns people most about long-term care, whether at home, in an assisted living facility, or in a nursing home, is how to pay for that care. There are basically five ways that you can pay for the cost of long-term care.

1. PAY WITH YOUR OWN FUNDS – This is the method many people are required to use at first. Quite simply, it means paying for the cost of long-term care out of your own pocket. Unfortunately, with nursing home bills averaging between $6,000 and $10,000 per month in some areas, few people can afford a long-term stay in a nursing home.

Many people will deplete their lifelong assets if they reside in a nursing home.

Some long-term care expenses can reach $20,000 or more per month if it is around-the-clock and in the home. Not only can few people afford to pay for a long-term care stay in a nursing home or in a residence, they can run out of money and assets in months, not years, and become impoverished quickly.

2. LONG-TERM CARE INSURANCE (LTCI) – If you are fortunate enough to have this type of coverage, it may go a long way toward paying the cost of long-term care either in your home, assisted living facility, or in the nursing home. Long-term care insurance can also help keep your family together and relieve stress. There is no other form of insurance that pays for nursing care in your home, the assisted living facility, or in a nursing home.

3. MEDICARE – This is the national health insurance program primarily for people 65 years of age and older, certain younger disabled people, and people with kidney failure. Medicare provides only short term and limited assistance with nursing home costs, but only if you meet the

strict qualification rules. It pays nothing for Skilled Nursing Care (SNF), only for rehabilitation.

4. MEDICAID – This is a federal- and state-funded and state-administered medical benefit program which can pay for the cost of the nursing home if certain asset and income requirements are met. Medicaid traditionally will only pay for the Skilled Nursing Facility (SNF), and in limited circumstances, some home care.

5. VETERANS ADMINISTRATION – The VA has a program called Aid & Attendance, which will pay veterans or their spouses for long-term care for non-military related illnesses such as Alzheimer's disease or Parkinson's disease if they meet certain requirements.

Too many people end up in a Skilled Nursing Facility (SNF) before they really have to because they, their spouses, partners, children, or advisors didn't know about the options, didn't plan, or didn't have the money or long-term care insurance to pay for care.

WHO DECIDES?

T here are a number of legal documents you will need to protect yourself and your assets. The following is a brief overview. These documents also apply when someone else is in need of care, such as a loved one. If you don't plan ahead, someone else will decide for you. The worst case is when the court appoints someone you don't know and who has no idea what your wishes are.

Remember Terri Schiavo?
Will you be the next Terri?

On February 25, 1990, Terri Schiavo, age 26, collapsed and had to stay in institutions in a vegetative state for 15 years. Terri's husband brought a petition to have her feeding tube removed. Terri's parents brought a countersuit requesting that the tube remain inserted so that Terri may continue living. The laws of the State of Florida were clear in that the decision in such an event is left to the spouse, and not the parents. It was irrelevant that Terri's spouse had since separated from her, was living with another woman, and had several children with her, because the law, as it was stated, did not void the spouse's rights in such circumstances. As a result, the state legislature, the governor of Florida, the US Congress, the president of the United States, and even the Pope all weighed in on the case. In the end, the letter of the law prevailed.

The saddest part in the Terri Schiavo case is that none of this had to happen. While we all know what Terri got, we will never know what she actually wanted. While it seems as though you will never become a Terri Schiavo, we are sure that Terri never thought she would be either. The problem was that everyone knew what Terri wanted, but since she never documented it, we'll never know.

The following section is provided for information purposes only; it is not legal advice. You must work with an attorney to implement the appropriate documents for you. Chapter Eight discusses how to find a qualified attorney who is knowledgeable in elder law.

MEDICAL POWER OF ATTORNEY OR HEALTH CARE PROXY

The alternative to all the state proceedings is to simply complete a proper healthcare directive and a living will. A healthcare proxy is also known as healthcare power of attorney or advanced health care directive. This is a document signed by an individual that authorizes another individual to have sole control over all healthcare decisions related to the incapacitated individual.

A Durable Power of Attorney for Healthcare (the name varies from state to state) empowers another person to make medical decisions for you if you become unable to make these decisions for yourself. If you have not designated someone of your choice as your attorney-in-fact or Personal Representative under HIPAA to make medical decisions for you, to be your advocate, the courts will act like they did for Terri Schiavo. If you don't decide and plan ahead with a Medical Power of Attorney, a stranger, estranged family member, or worse, the government, could decide your fate. Not having a properly executed Health Care Directive can make you the next Terri.

Planning Tip:
How to Survive a Hospital Stay

In his book, *Cancer as a Turning Point*, Lawrence Leshan said that the way to survive a hospital stay is to have an advocate by your bedside to question everything. Who better than your spouse, partner, adult child, or person of your choice?

Without a current Durable Medical Power of Attorney and HIPAA Declaration your spouse, partner, sibling, adult child, parent, etc., won't be your advocate and certainly won't be your Personal Representative under HIPAA rules.

A common mistake people make is bringing family members to meetings with their medical care providers and then they assume the care providers will honor the family member as the Personal Representative. As I found out with a major hospital recently, this is not so. If you want the care provider(s) to give information to your Personal Representative, you must have a current Advance Health Directive on file with the care provider and a HIPAA Declaration also on file. Your attorney can advise you on this. Once you have these documents on file, it is a violation of federal law if the care provider refuses or fails to provide the information you and your family have every right to know!

You should always carry this document with you when you travel or in your glove compartment.

Planning Tip:
The Smart Way to Have your Medical Powers Always Available

Since "normal" people don't walk around with their medical power of attorney, keep it in their glove compartment, or remember to take it when they travel, there is an easier, smarter, and safer way to handle this.

The website www.docubank.com provides an online service for maintaining your legal documents no matter where you are in the world as long as you or your health provider can access the Internet. Your membership number and password are on the membership card if your care provider needs access to the information in your Medical Power of Attorney.

WHO DECIDES MONEY MATTERS?

FINANCIAL POWER OF ATTORNEY

A Financial Power of Attorney is a document authorizing another individual to handle financial and legal matters on your behalf. A Power of Attorney is valid when signed and delivered to the person (agent) authorized to act on your behalf. There are Durable and Non-Durable Powers of Attorney. A Non-Durable Power of Attorney will cease to be valid upon your incapacity or incompetence. A Durable Power of Attorney will remain valid after your incapacity or incompetence.

Many states also offer a Springing Power of Attorney which takes effect upon the happening of an event you identify. Typically, the event relates to your incapacity or incompetence.

A very important limitation on Powers of Attorneys is that they terminate at your death. Your Agent is NOT AUTHORIZED TO ACT ON YOUR BEHALF AFTER YOUR DEATH. Powers of Attorney are very powerful documents that authorize people to act on your behalf without your oversight. A Power of Attorney, however, is extremely important to avoid the expensive legal proceedings that will appoint someone in the event of your incapacity or incompetence. A careful balance must be monitored to ensure the authority without granting unlimited authority which can be abused when you are not able to oversee your agent's activities. This document must have special "frailty" language. (Please see Chapter Seven: Preventing Elder Financial Abuse.)

LAST WILL AND TESTAMENT

A Last Will and Testament is a declaration by an individual directing where your assets are to be distributed after your death. In addition, it also names the individual (Executor) who is responsible to carry out the decedent's wishes. In most jurisdictions, for a Will to be validated (or "proven"), and for the terms of the Will to be carried out, it must go through a legal process called Probate. Remember, a will does not help if you don't die.

LIVING WILL

A Living Will is a document that identifies your personal wishes with regard to life-sustaining treatment in the event of your severe incapacity (i.e., comatose or vegetative state). In most cases, the Living Will merely outlines general instructions on the care you wish to receive (or not receive) in life or death situations. For example, in the Terri Schiavo case, a Living Will would have provided explicit instructions whether Terri wanted to be kept alive by tubular feeding. Other typical provisions in Living Wills generally identify your willingness to be kept alive by CPR, artificial respiration, tube feeding, or other heroic measures, if you are in a terminal, comatose, or vegetative condition. Instructions not involving life and death situations are usually provided for in a Personal Care Plan.

In some states, like California, the Medical Power of Attorney and the Living Will are combined in a document called the Advanced Health Care Directive.

PERSONAL CARE PLAN

A Personal Care Plan is an extensively detailed instruction outlining your wishes for your or a loved one's care in the event you or they are unable to express them and are in need of long-term care. Personal Care Plans often include specific instructions about your willingness regarding your desire to stay at home rather than being placed in a nursing home or other facility, and ensure the care you receive is appropriate based upon your financial means and your personal desires. They often go into such detail as daily hygiene and appearance, the food you like to eat, places you would like to visit, conditions for visitations, access to spiritual or religious clergy, books, TV, sports, hobbies, and many other personal desires of the individual.

REVOCABLE LIVING TRUST

A Revocable Living Trust is a contract creating a separate legal entity (called a Trust) that acts as your alter ego. In essence, an individual creates a Living Trust and transfers title of all their assets into the name of the Trust.

While alive, you can maintain full control and access to all of your assets in the Trust as you did when they were in your own name by acting as "Trustee" of the Trust. The difference, however, is in the event of your disability or death, the Trust has instructions to guide successor trustees (those you name, similar to an Executor in a Will) to provide for your needs and manage your assets in a manner you provide.

In the event of your death, the Trust terms will provide specific instructions to your Trustee on where to distribute your assets upon your passing. A Trust, when properly drawn, can serve as your set of instructions and allow your loved ones to avoid the state's "default" or "intestacy" laws.

A good Revocable Living Trust will provide extensive instructions as to who is in control of your assets when you are not able to be, how they are to use them for you and others you identify, and how they are to be distributed to those you love after your death.

Since this book is concerned with Long-Term Care, a living trust serves another purpose and it MUST have language in it that allows the trustee to make gifts or implement planning strategies should you need long-term care. Many trusts only focus on death or limit who can sign as a trustee. With people living longer and long-term care an issue, the trust language must be current and appropriate for your situation today. Many old trusts fail to have current HIPAA language, making the trust much less effective. Having a living trust alone will not protect your assets if you need long-term care.

IRREVOCABLE TRUST

The significance of an Irrevocable Trust is that once it is created, it typically cannot be amended or altered. Traditionally, Irrevocable Trusts do not permit the creator to have any control or access to the assets in it. In addition, the creator is unable to change the beneficiaries or the terms of the Trust. The primary purpose of these types of Trusts is to avoid high taxes at death and/or asset protection against lawsuits, or other predators during life.

Since the extensive changes in asset protection and estate tax laws have occurred over the last 10 years, new types of Irrevocable Trusts are now much friendlier. For example, Irrevocable Trusts still can be used to maintain asset protection without having to give up control of your assets and without you having to give up the income from assets put in them. In fact, in some cases, you can even retain full use of your assets for the rest of your life, without them being at risk of being lost to lawsuits, nursing homes, or other creditors or predators. These trusts have become a very important tool in long-term care planning, as we will see in Chapters Two, Three, Four and Six.

HAD ENOUGH LEGALESE?

The point of all this legal mumbo-jumbo is if your documents do not exist, are not current, or do not address what happens if you need long-term care, then you, like Terri, will not be in charge of your life! It's time to see an elder law attorney, especially if Medicaid or VA benefits are involved, as we will see in Chapters Three, Four, and Six.

AVOIDING A FAMILY CRISIS

A Not–So Unusual Family Story

Let's visit Paul, who was happily married to Helen, a stay-at-home mom raising their 5-year-old son. Helen realized that after her mother died, her father, Jack, was losing his memory and was unable to care for himself. So she asked her husband if Jack could move in with them. Not understanding what they were getting into or that there were alternatives, Paul agreed.

Jack's entire estate planning assumed he would die first and never considered an extended disability. When Jack's wife died, he was devastated. When asked how he was doing, he said, "Fine."

Over the next several months, Jack started wandering and had mood changes, delusions, and hallucinations. The stress level from his erratic behavior was so great that the two of them were arguing all the time. Divorce was being discussed. Paul's successful business was in chaos because Paul, an expert witness in his field, had to cancel one trip after another to support Helen.

Is this unusual? Not really. Is this the best way to go? Absolutely not! What saved Paul and Helen was luck. Helen's siblings stepped in and had Jack move in with them. The tragedy is not what happened, but that it could have been avoided.

The way you avoid a family a crisis is through good communication. The worksheet on the next page should help you before a family crisis occurs. Many times children are unwilling to talk to their parents because they think their parents will think they are after their money. If you don't address these questions directly with your loved ones, you could end up like Paul and Helen and pay for their long-term care; impoverishing them and yourself. The funds you were hoping to help with your retirement or your children's education can disappear very quickly. The tragedy is that it may be avoided. Have courage, speak to your loved ones, and ask away. Adult children must involve their parents in this discussion NOW. You must take the step and start the conversation NOW.

AVOIDING A FAMILY CRISIS WORKSHEET

Asking these questions of your loved ones is the first step in avoiding a family financial crisis. You must start the process NOW. The second step is taking action.

1. Do you have enough assets to sustain a healthy spouse if one of you needs an extended hospitalization, care at home, or an assisted living facility or nursing home? _____

_____

2. How much income do you have? Is it enough to maintain your standard of living? What does your income look like? What happens to your income when one of the spouses dies? _____

_____

3. Do you have enough to pay for long-term care that continues for one year, two years, three years, or longer? _____

_____

4. What types of insurance do you have? How much do they pay and when? _____

_____

5. Are your legal documents current and in alignment, or are they stale and out of date? Do they have frailty language? _____

_____

6. Do you have a Will and is it current? Do you have a Health Care Directive and Power of Attorney? _____

_____

And, most importantly, the same questions apply to you, too!

Chapter Two

15 Medicaid Mistakes to Avoid

There is no terror in a bang, only in the anticipation of it.
-Alfred Hitchcock

Remember when Mom said, "Do not do this!" or your first grade teacher said, "Do not do this!" Well, here we are.

People make costly and unnecessary mistakes when they are desperate. Here are some of the most frequent to avoid.

1. Giving away assets without talking to an elder law attorney and assuming the kids will take care of you.

One of the most common do-it-yourself strategies is to just give assets away. Giving assets away without understanding Medicaid ramifications or without working with a qualified elder law attorney could be financially devastating.

2. Assuming the annuity you bought will protect you from Medicaid.

Many people bought annuities believing that their annuity would protect their assets and help them qualify for Medicaid. This may have been the case before 2006, but the Deficit Reduction Act (DRA) has made most annuities no longer effective with respect to Medicaid. There are some new annuities (referred to as DRA Medicaid-Compliant) that may protect assets when used properly.

3. Attempting to hide assets from Medicaid.

We live in the Internet age and it is no longer possible or realistic to hide assets from Medicaid. You may "forget" to mention an asset or that you transferred property away, but Medicaid will probably discover it. The failure to disclose assets in order to obtain Medicaid is a crime and could result in legal action to recover Medicaid benefits.

4. WAITING TOO LONG TO TAKE ACTION.

It's a mistake to sit back and do nothing when a loved one is either in a nursing home or in need of nursing care. The longer you wait, the deeper into crisis you get. It's never too late to plan. If you are in a crisis and feel you are out of options, you must talk to a qualified elder law attorney (see Chapter Eight).

5. DEPENDING ON NON-PROFESSIONAL ADVICE.

It is amazing how many people who wouldn't make a financial move without talking to their financial advisor would ask a neighbor, friend, relative, insurance broker, stock broker, or accountant—anyone except a qualified Medicaid specialist. Talking to someone who is not qualified, whether it is about Medicaid, Medi-Cal, or Mass Health can be a very costly mistake resulting in the loss of thousands or hundreds of thousands of dollars.

6. TAKING ADVICE OF THE MEDICAID WORKER.

Would you call the IRS for tax advice? This is worse. You can amend or correct bad tax advice. With Medicaid, you could be disqualified or penalized with no option of recovery, or spend down your money or assets unnecessarily because of incorrect or incomplete information, or because you asked the wrong question. Medicaid rules are very complex and require specialized knowledge by professionals who practice in the field regularly.

7. ASSUMING MEDICARE IS THE SAME AS MEDICAID.

Medicare pays for acute care that leads to rehabilitation or getting better. Medicaid pays for long-term care in the nursing home and sometimes for home care, depending on your state's Medicaid plan. Medicare is administered all over the country in the same way. Medicaid is administered by individual states and can differ from state to state.

8. PICKING THE WRONG ATTORNEY.

Many times when the need for long-term care strikes, your first stop is the attorney's office. What you need to do is talk to an attorney who really focuses exclusively in this area of care. Medicaid is a highly specialized area requiring an understanding of Medicaid, VA benefits, estate law, and tax law. In Chapter Eight we will discuss how to identify the right elder law attorney for you and provide resources.

9. BELIEVING YOU CAN JUST GIVE $13,000 AWAY.

Medicaid law and tax law are very different. It is true that the tax code allows you to give up to $13,000 away every year to any number of people. Medicaid, however, assumes that you are trying to qualify for Medicaid when you give money away. So, if you give your grandchild a gift to help pay for college, years later, when you may need Medicaid, you could be disqualified or penalized from Medicaid because they look at it differently than you and the tax code.

10. APPLYING FOR MEDICAID TOO SOON.

It is a mistake to apply for Medicaid just to see if "it will fly" or if "you will qualify" because once you apply, your private information about your assets and investments is no longer private. The strategies that could apply as you will read in Chapter Three or when you work with an elder law attorney may no longer be available because you spilled your beans.[15]

11. ASSUMING A LIVING TRUST WILL PROTECT ASSETS FROM MEDICAID.

A properly drawn living trust can provide many benefits; unfortunately,

---

15 My former sales training coach, Jim Camp, used to say, "Never, never spill your beans, because you can't pick them up," or something to that effect.

protecting your assets from Medicaid is not one of them. Assets in a revocable living trust are available to the patient and, therefore, are available as countable assets to Medicaid. Unless the living trust has "frailty" language in it, then the well spouse or trustee may not be able to access the assets in the trust should the patient be in a nursing home or severely disabled and unable to act on his or her behalf.

12. MAKING TRANSFERS WITHOUT PROPER AUTHORITY.

Sometimes, in a family's desperation to protect assets for a family member who is no longer mentally competent or severely disabled, they will transfer assets without proper legal authority to do so. This may be considered elder abuse. A good-intentioned social worker, hospital worker, nurse, or family member will report you to Adult Protective Services (APS). This is the last thing that you need. A qualified elder law attorney could prevent this problem and protect you.

13. SPENDING DOWN INTO POVERTY.

The law does not say you must spend down into poverty to qualify for Medicaid. It says you must meet strict income and asset requirements. You can take advantage of safe harbors and transfers created by Congress. You can take steps with the help of an elder law attorney to protect your spouse or children in certain situations. We will discuss these and more in Chapter Three.

14. MOM HAS ALZHEIMER'S DISEASE! WE BETTER GET A REVERSE MORTGAGE!

Bad idea! As we will see in the next chapter, the home can be an exempt or a non-counted asset when it comes to Medicaid. The money you receive from the reverse mortgage is not an exempt asset. Also, once you leave the home permanently, the reverse mortgage must be paid off.

A reverse mortgage, on the other hand, may make sense where Medicaid is not an option or won't be needed. Or where the value of the equity in the house exceeds $500,000 or $750,000 in some states and you need to bring the equity down to qualify for Medicaid. A home equity loan can also be used to reduce equity. You will want to review these issues with an elder law attorney.

15. MOM IS SICK. WE'LL SELL HER HOUSE TO PAY FOR HER NURSING HOME CARE.

The home may be protected as an exempt asset but the proceeds from selling the house are not protected. It makes more sense to see an elder law attorney who can help Mom qualify for Medicaid, then deal with the house.

In the next chapter we will discuss what you need to know about Medicaid, what's protected, and what's not protected.

CHAPTER THREE
UNDERSTANDING MEDICAID

"Government is the great fiction, through which everybody endeavors to live at the expense of everybody else."

-Frédéric Bastiat

A person facing the prospect of long-term care with moderate income and assets may eventually have to rely on Medicaid for all or part of the cost. Medicaid is an extremely complex and confusing benefit. The purpose of this chapter is to serve as a guide to help you better understand Medicaid and the issues you face. Neither the author nor the publisher is engaged in the practice of law. Should you decide to act on any of the information in this chapter, you will need to work with qualified legal counsel before taking any action.[16]

CRISIS PLANNING

When you have no money and you or a loved one needs long-term care, you are in a crisis. When you are at your wits end and you are paying out of pocket for you or your loved one's long-term care, you are in a crisis. When you think you have no options or when your spouse has just gone into a care facility and you think you have to sell the house or get a reverse mortgage you are in a crisis. The list goes on.

As we said in the very beginning, you never want to be in crisis, but we live in a real world. And crisis is what happens in real life to real people. Medicaid has become the insurer of last resort in a skilled nursing home (SNF) to middle income people to pay for long-term care.

---

16 Information in this chapter has been initially derived from www.ElderLawAnwsers.com and reviewed and updated by David J. Zumpano, CPA and Attorney in New York *(www.eplawcenter. com)* and Bob Scrivano, Sacramento, CA. 2010.

MEDICAID OVERVIEW

Simply put, Medicaid is a benefits program primarily funded by the federal government and administered by the state that pays for health and long-term care for eligible citizens and legal residents. Since Medicaid covers more than just the elderly, we will only focus on long-term care. Unlike Medicare, Medicaid is needs-based and you must meet strict income and asset guidelines. The federal government sets the guidelines and states have some rights to modify them.

One of the major problems with Medicaid is that it is not only administered differently from state to state, but can be administered differently from county to county, and even from worker to worker. It's not even called Medicaid in a number of states. For example:

In California, it's Medi-Cal.
In Massachusetts, it's MassHealth
In Arizona, it's ALTCS or Arizona Long-Term Care System

Confusion rules the day, especially when it comes to Medicaid and when your loved ones needing care live in another state.

Today most people end up paying for long-term care out of their own pocket until they run of money and life savings. Then they expect the government to pick up the cost. The advantage of paying privately is that you have a choice and you don't have to deal with the state's Medicaid bureaucracy, or at least you can put it off. The disadvantage is that it is very expensive; $35,000 to $150,000 depending on where you receive the care.[17] (Appendix A illustrates costs in various American cities.)

Careful planning, whether in advance, in response to an anticipated need, or in crisis, can help protect your estate for you and your loved ones. You can purchase long-term care insurance (Chapter Five) or make sure that you receive all the benefits you are entitled to by working with a qualified elder law attorney (Chapter Eight). Veterans and their spouses may seek help from the Veterans Administration, as we will discuss in Chapter Four.

---

17 *www.elderlawanwers.com*, 2010.

What about Medicare?

There is a great deal of confusion about Medicare and Medicaid. Medicare is the federally-funded and state-administered health insurance program primarily for individuals 65 or older, or individuals under age 65, but deemed disabled for two years.

Medicare is essentially health insurance for the elderly. Generally, after an individual reaches age 65 and qualifies for Social Security, he or she will also be eligible for Medicare healthcare benefits. Medicare has two parts: Part A and Part B. Part A covers all the costs of hospital stays, doctor visits, and hospital examinations. Part B covers costs for exams, MRI scans, X-rays, and the like. Part D covers the cost of prescriptions. A supplemental plan covers doctor visits. Since Medicare does not cover long-term care, we are not going to spend a lot of time on Medicare.

**Major Differences Between
Medicare and Medicaid**

Medicare	Medicaid
- Pays for acute care where rehabilitation is possible	-Pays for chronic/custodial care where patient will not get better
- Administered uniformly throughout the United States	-Administered differently in each state
- Application automatic at age 65 once registered	-Applicant must meet strict income and asset requirements, and in some cases, age requirements

When it comes to Medicare, there is considerable information available on the Internet, Consumer Reports, insurance companies, AARP, Medicare, and the Social Security Administration. The only real similarity between the two is the spelling; both start with "Medi." Please don't get confused—they are NOT THE SAME. This chapter focuses on Medicaid and how it may pay for you or your loved one's long-term care.

Medicare pays very limited benefits for long-term care. Essentially, Medicare will only pay the first 20 days of a stay at a skilled nursing facility, but only if certain conditions are met. First, admission to a hospital must have been for at least three days (defined by Medicare as three midnights). Second, the individual must have entered a nursing home within 30 days of their discharge from the hospital, and third, the stay in the nursing home must be rehabilitative. Medicare will only pay for rehabilitative care, not custodial care. If rehabilitative care continues beyond the 20 days, Medicare then only pays that amount over a mandated co-payment required to be paid by the individual. Currently, this amount is $141.50 (2011). Therefore, if a cost of a nursing home was $241.50 per day, Medicare will pay $100, and the individual is responsible for $141.50 for each day they stay in the nursing home from days 21 through 100.

Many health insurance policies have provisions to cover this co-payment during days 21 through 100. You should check with your health insurance provider to determine whether or not your policy provides for it. Should you not have supplemental insurance, you will be responsible for the co-payment each day of your admission.

Lastly, it is important to note that Medicare can stop paying at any time if it is determined you are no longer being rehabilitated, or have reached the maximum amount of rehabilitation. Medicare, however, must give you 24 hours notice of its intention to terminate its coverage. Assuming rehabilitation is continued under the terms, the maximum Medicare benefit would expire at the end of the 100th day.

Planning Tip

If you are assuming that Medicare will pay for long term care, chronic conditions, or because you don't have long-term care insurance, or don't have the money to pay for care, the bad news in the real world is that Medicare, on average, does not pay for more than seven or eight days. If you are hospitalized with a chronic illness, it will pay the amount over $141.50 or the current co-pay per day for days 21 through 100.

The only other federal benefit program available to pay for nursing home care is Medicaid, and, if you qualify, the VA may also help pay. The rest of this chapter will focus on Medicaid. When you run out of options or money, understanding Medicaid and knowing where to get help becomes critical.

MEDICAID AND THE ATTORNEY

Do you really need an attorney when it comes to Medicaid? This depends on your situation. Whether you are in a crisis or are planning ahead, the prudent answer is probably "yes." The social worker at your mother's nursing home may not even want you or a loved one in the facility on Medicaid and is often not aware of all the particulars of your situation, what's new in the law, or how Medicaid is administered in your county. The worst that could happen for the price of a consultation with a qualified professional who looks at your total situation is peace of mind or help you or a loved one get into an appropriate nursing home.

Planning Tip:
How a Little Error Can Be Very Costly

Bill Hammond, an elder law attorney in Kansas, speaks of a client who was a highly-skilled professional accountant. This client was trained in income tax, gift tax, estate tax, and governmental audits of finances. This "highly-skilled" accountant whose mother needed Medicaid benefits read and analyzed the written regulations of Medicaid in his state.

He used his understanding of tax law to interpret the facts. He then took action to save $500,000 by transferring it to an irrevocable trust. Then he began paying for his mother's care for what he determined was the Medicaid waiting period. Finally, he filled out a Medicaid application and submitted it. While he was filling out the application, he checked an innocent box which asked a seemingly obvious question: "Do you wish to apply for all Medicaid benefits to which you are entitled?" He answered "yes." As it turned out, that was the wrong answer.

"Yes" seemed like the right answer in this case. After all, why wouldn't you apply for all the benefits available to you? Because of his mother's specific set of circumstances, the Medicaid

---

application was not submitted at the right time. So the Medicaid department in his state counted the $500,000 transfer as a gift, resulting in a penalty period of ineligibility of 100 months.

A "little" error is easy to make by anyone who does not work in the area of Medicaid on a regular basis. This is why it is recommended that you work with a qualified elder law attorney. Chapter Eight describes the steps that will help you identify the appropriate attorney for you.

Planning Tip:
Qualifying when Others Have Said Not Possible

David J. Zumpano, attorney and CPA, who focuses on elder law and estate planning in New York, speaks of a client who called him to determine if they qualified for Medicaid. They had seen their regular attorney who said that since Dad had $400,000, Mom would not qualify for Medicaid to pay for her stay in a nursing home for her Alzheimer's disease.

Interestingly, the client's regular attorney told them substantially all of their assets would be lost, but after meeting with Dave, he was able to get the client qualified for Medicaid immediately, even with the amount of assets they had. The reason was that the client qualified for a little-known exception under the Medicaid law which made her eligible immediately, even with the community spouse having a home and over $400,000 of assets.

Obviously, it is critically important that the attorney you work with when you need Medicaid is fully informed on the Medicaid issues and does this on a regular and extensive basis.

THE RULES

Medicaid rules are like doing a giant jigsaw puzzle on the beach; the sand is shifting, the wind is blowing, and the tide is coming in. Of course, you could move away from the edge and use a table or do the puzzle on the boardwalk.

There are basically two Medicaid principles with respect to married couples when one spouse needs nursing home care. The first principle is that spouses are financially responsible for one another. The assets of the well spouse, also called the community spouse, are viewed as available to the ill spouse in the nursing home. The second principal is that you don't want to impoverish the well spouse by spending all their money and assets on the ill spouse.

Medicaid qualification rules, therefore, fall into two major areas: assets and income, and they are different for singles and married people. Remember, "married" to Medicaid means traditional marriage to a partner of a different gender. Legal separation is still counted as married by Medicaid.

Congress doesn't want you to give your assets away one day and then apply for Medicaid the next day. Unfortunately, when President Bush signed the Deficit Reduction Act (DRA) into law on February 8, 2006, qualifying for Medicaid became much more restrictive. The purpose of the DRA was to cut nearly $40 billion over five years from Medicare, Medicaid, and other programs.[18]

What does this mean to you—a baby boomer and your aging loved ones? It means that there are now significant restrictions on obtaining Medicaid to help pay for the health care you or your loved ones may need. The only way the government can control the expansion of Medicaid is by making it more difficult to get.

18 *www.ElderLawAnswers.com* 2010.

To qualify for Medicaid, you must pass strict tests on income and the assets that you can keep. To understand how Medicaid works, we first need to review what are known as "exempt" or "non-countable" and "non-exempt" or "countable" assets. We will also review income requirements in Part II.

PART I: ASSET RULES

The starting point in understanding the asset rules for married couples is that all assets owned by either spouse are considered available to the nursing home spouse for purposes of Medicaid. Some assets are treated as non-countable assets while other assets are counted. Assets cannot be left out of the picture on the basis that they belong exclusively to the spouse who is not applying for Medicaid.

The following two lists are general federal guidelines; the specific rules for your state may differ. All assets are counted unless they fall within the following list of non-countable assets. In general, the following are primary "exempt" or "non-countable" assets:

NON-COUNTABLE (EXEMPT) ASSETS

◎ For a single-person home equity up to $500,000 (some states go up to $750,000). For married people, the full value of the house may be protected if the healthy (community) spouse lives in the home.[19] The home must be the principal place of residence. You may be required to show "intent to return home" or prove likelihood of returning home, depending on your state, even if this never actually takes place. In some states you can use assessed value.[20]

---

19 If the community spouse dies first, the home is subject to state recovery if the home is not transferred out of the nursing home spouse's name. In this case, the protection is really temporary or a delay until the state recovers its cost for the institutionalized spouse, unless you are living in a Homestead State. If the community spouse dies after the institutionalized spouse, then there is no recovery. Your elder law attorney will have to guide you in that case.
20 In some states, if you are single, it's exempt up to the limits. If you fail to reside in the house for a certain of number of months, it's not exempt. Your elder law attorney will guide you.

⊚ Personal belongings and household goods

⊚ Jewelry up to $100 in value

⊚ One car or truck

⊚ Burial spaces and certain related items for applicant and spouse

⊚ Irrevocable prepaid funeral contract or funeral trust for applicant, spouse. or other qualified family member

⊚ Value of life insurance if face value is $1,500 or less. If it does exceed $1,500 in total face amount, then the cash value in these policies is countable.

⊚ Term insurance

⊚ Life insurance in an Irrevocable Life Insurance Trust (ILIT) if transferred or created prior to look-back period

⊚ Life insurance on you owned by somebody else

⊚ Business property depending on your states rules

⊚ IRAs have special rules. See the Q&A at the end of this chapter.

All other assets are generally non-exempt and are countable. Without proper planning, an "exempt" asset, such as one's home, may become a "non-exempt" asset and be counted.

Basically, all money and property, and any item that can be valued and turned into cash, is a countable asset unless it is one of those assets listed above as exempt.

COUNTABLE (NON-EXEMPT) ASSETS

⊚ Cash, savings, and checking accounts, credit union share and draft accounts

⊚ Certificates of deposit

⊚ US savings bonds

⊚ Nursing home accounts

⊚ Prepaid funeral contracts which can be canceled

⊚ Assets in Revocable Living Trusts

⊚ Real estate (other than the residence)

⊚ More than one car

⊚ Boats or recreational vehicles

⊚ Stocks, bonds, or mutual funds

⊚ Land contracts or mortgages held on real estate sold

⊚ Promissory notes if they don't meet Medicaid requirements

⊚ Annuities if they don't meet requirements

⊚ 529 Plans depending on your state.

Planning Tip:
Why the Funeral Trust

If you have CDs, life insurance cash value, or investments you are saving for funeral expenses, the way to avoid having those assets counted is to put it or them into a Funeral Trust. A Funeral Trust is single-use trust funded by an irrevocable life insurance policy. You deposit the amount you want to protect up to $12,500 and Medicaid, the nursing home, creditors, or predators cannot touch it. (The maximum may be different in your state.)

While Medicaid rules themselves are complicated and tricky, it's safe to say that a single person will qualify for Medicaid as long as she has only exempt assets plus a small amount of cash and/or money in the bank. The current law states you may not exceed $2,000 (in most states). However, if you have more than $2,000 in countable assets, that does not mean a good legal advocate could not help you qualify.

COMMUNITY SPOUSE RESOURCE ALLOWANCE (CSRA)

After adding together all of your countable marital assets, your state's Medicaid agency will then determine what share of those assets you, if you're the healthy spouse, will be allowed to keep while your spouse in the nursing home receives Medicaid benefits. This amount is based on a combination of federal and state laws called the Community Spouse Resource Allowance (CSRA).

Your CSRA is equal to half of the total joint assets you and your spouse have on the day you become institutionalized. Your CSRA, however, is limited to an amount between $21,912 and $109,560, and these amounts are adjusted annually by the federal government (See Appendix B).

The effect of the CSRA is to reduce the assets that are considered available for the nursing home spouse. For example, let's say you are a couple who has a combined $300,000 in countable assets. If you live in a state that allows the spouse to keep the maximum $109,560, all of the rest of the assets will need to go toward the cost of care for the nursing home spouse. If the amount of assets is less than your state's maximum, then nothing will be used for Medicaid. The problem is that the amount and how it's calculated can be different from state to state.

An elder law attorney may be able to help you protect some of those assets and convert them to non-countable assets.

**Planning Tip:
The Partnership for LTCi can increase the Amount Protected**

In Chapter Five, one of the forms of long term care insurance we will discuss is the Partnership for LTC Insurance. Had you owned the PLTC insurance, the Partnership plan would protect the full $300,000 and not just the $109,560 as defined by the CSRA.

PART II: TREATMENT OF INCOME

Income is treated differently from assets for married couples. Unlike assets, the income of the well spouse (community spouse) is not considered available to the spouse in the nursing home. There are provisions in the Medicaid rules for using income from the nursing home spouse to support the community spouse, but not vice-versa. The income that belongs to the community spouse that is totally separate is always theirs to keep.

As a general rule, the income of the nursing home spouse must go to the nursing home to pay for care. There are, however, a few exceptions that protect the well spouse and are calculated as deductions from the cost of care. A small amount may be set aside as a personal needs allowance. This amount generally ranges from $30 to $75 per month, depending on which state you live in.

A single person in California, for example, is allowed to keep $35 per month for expenses. But if that person lives in New York, she can keep $50 a month.

Income from the nursing home spouse can be given to the community spouse or to dependent children if their separate income is not enough to meet their needs. In the case of dependent children, each child may receive an amount equal to one half of the Federal Poverty Level for a single adult, which was $1,133.00 per month in 2011.

Medicaid provides a minimum income standard for the community spouse called the "Minimum Monthly Maintenance Needs Allowance" or MMMNA. This provision is set at one and a half times (1.5x) the Federal Poverty Level for a single person living alone. By using the MMMNA, Medicaid is attempting to prevent impoverishing the community spouse in cases where the community spouse's income is less than the MMMNA. The current MMMNA is between $1,821 and $2,739 per month depending on what state you live in.

The amount of MMMNA can be increased in a special hearing where you must prove that your expenses are more than the minimum allowance.

Planning Tip

In Chapter Five we will discuss long-term care insurance, and in particular, the Partnership for Long-Term Care Insurance. An important benefit of long-term care insurance is that it can protect the income of the well spouse by paying for the needs of the nursing home spouse, independent of their income or assets.

The Partnership Plan can not only provide the care payment until benefits are exhausted, it can also protect the assets from Medicaid, as we will see in Chapter Five. However, it does not protect income after benefits are exhausted.

The deeper we get into this, the more complicated it gets. An elder law attorney who understands the particulars of your situation can determine how much MMMNA you qualify for, and what the best strategy is for you.

MEDICAID QUESTIONS & ANSWERS

1. CAN I GIVE MY ASSETS AWAY?

Maybe, but only if it's done just right. The law has severe penalties for people who simply give away their assets to create Medicaid eligibility. Even though the Federal Gift Tax laws allow you to give away up to $13,000 per year to any number of people without gift tax consequences, these gifts could result in a period of ineligibility for Medicaid, otherwise known as the Transfer Penalty.

2. ARE THERE EXCEPTIONS TO THE TRANSFER PENALTY?

We've discussed that transferring property creates penalties which can delay an application for Medicaid eligibility. There are a number of exceptions to the transfer penalty rule that may work in your case, if you transfer property to:

- A spouse
- Anyone else as long as it's for the spouse's benefit
- A blind or disabled child
- A trust for the benefit of a blind or disabled child
- A gift that is less than your state's average monthly cost of care in one month

3. ARE THERE EXCEPTIONS IF I TRANSFER MY HOME?

There are special exceptions that apply to the transfer of a home. The Medicaid applicant may freely transfer his or her home to the following individuals without incurring a transfer penalty:

- The applicant's spouse[22]

---

22 There are exceptions and special rules for Homestead States

◎ A child who is under age 21, or who is blind or disabled

◎ A trust for the sole benefit of an individual who is disabled under the age of 65

◎ A sibling who has lived in the house during the year preceding the applicant's institutionalization who already holds an equity interest in the house

◎ A caretaker child who is defined as a child of the applicant who lived in the house at least two years prior to the applicant's institutionalization and who, during that period, provided care that allowed the applicant to avoid a nursing home stay.[23]

Planning Tip

Let's suppose that you are living in your mother's house and taking care of her. If you've been doing this for two (2) years or longer, she can transfer the house to you without a penalty.

---

4. I'M SINGLE. HOW MUCH INCOME CAN I KEEP?

If you are single and applying for Medicaid, the most income you can have is $35 per month. In some states, it's higher—up to $75 per month and $2,000 in assets—that's it.

Planning Tip

If you're single and have Social Security and IRA income, anything over the $35 (or whatever it is in your state) would go toward the cost of care before Medicaid pays. While your IRA is a non-counted or exempt asset, the income is not.

You could, as we'll see later, use an immediate annuity inside your IRA.

---

23 *www.elderlawanswers.com*

5. I'M MARRIED. HOW MUCH INCOME CAN I KEEP?

Each state also establishes a monthly income limit for the at-home spouse. This is called the Minimum Monthly Maintenance Needs Allowance (MMMNA). This permits the community spouse to keep a minimum monthly income of $2,739 (minimum is $1,821). See Appendix C for the list per state for 2011. If the community spouse does not have at least $2,739 in income, then he or she is allowed to take the income of the nursing home spouse in an amount large enough to reach the Minimum Monthly Maintenance Needs Allowance. The nursing home spouse's remaining income goes to the nursing home. You may be able to raise this amount by court order.

Can you live on $2,739 per month? This is where the pedal hits the metal and you need qualified legal help and to do some pre-planning with a qualified financial advisor.

Planning Tip:
Beware

Federal law requires that when the spouse's income exceeds MMMNA, 25 percent of that income must go to cost of care for the institutionalized spouse. As of this writing, only New York State enforces this.

Word to the Wise: As states recognize that their Medicaid funding is inadequate, they could enforce this rule to raise money. They may also start enforcing their filial laws addressed in Question 15. You must plan ahead for these contingencies.

6. I'M IN A NON-MARRIED RELATIONSHIP. HOW MUCH MONEY CAN I KEEP?

Both of you are considered single.

7. HOW CAN I PROTECT MY HEALTHY SPOUSE'S ASSETS?

In general, the community spouse can keep one half of the couple's total countable assets up to a maximum of $109,560 (in 2011). This is called the Community Spouse Resource Allowance, or CSRA. The amount in your state could be different. The least that a state can allow a community spouse to retain is $21,912 (in 2011). The healthy spouses' separate exempt assets are always separate and are not available to Medicaid.

8. WHAT HAPPENS IF I LIVE OFF MY HUSBAND'S INCOME AND HE GOES TO A NURSING HOME?

If you are the community spouse, you are entitled to some or all of your husband's income. How much you will get depends on your state's Medicaid agency. What you will get is known as the "minimum monthly maintenance needs allowance" or MMMNA. MMMNA is calculated according to a complicated formula based on your housing costs and may range from $1,821.50 to $2,739 per month (2011). If your income falls below the MMMNA, the shortfall is made up from your spouse's income.

9. WHAT IS ESTATE RECOVERY?

Estate recovery does not take place until the recipient of the benefits dies (or until both spouses are deceased if it is a married couple). Then, federal law requires that states attempt to recover the benefits paid from the recipient's probate estate and, in some cases, non-probate estate. Generally, the probate estate consists of assets that the deceased owned in his or her name alone without beneficiary designation. This includes revocable trusts. The non-probate assets include assets owned jointly or payable to a beneficiary.

About two-thirds of the nation's nursing home residents have their costs paid in part by Medicaid. The Estate Recovery law obviously affects many families. The asset most frequently caught in the Estate Recovery web is the home of the Medicaid recipient. A nursing home resident can often own a home and receive Medicaid benefits without having to sell the home.

Confused? Let's look at this again. If the home goes from the spouse on Medicaid in the nursing home to the other spouse and the spouse on Medicaid dies first, there is no right of recovery.

Planning Tip:
Protecting your House from Recovery

If you are working with an elder law attorney, you might be able to protect your home from Estate Recovery with one of the transfer exceptions and the use of an irrevocable trust. The attorney can guide you in this area.

10. DO I HAVE TO USE MY IRA FOR COST OF CARE IF I GO TO A NURSING HOME AND NEED MEDICAID?

Your IRA is a special situation. It is available as a non-exempt asset. However, if you have a Medicaid qualified annuity which means it has been annuitized based on your life expectancy, then if you die before your life expectancy, the remaining income can go to someone else. There is no requirement that the balance has to go to the state. There may be exceptions in your state that an elder law attorney can help you with.

11. DO I HAVE TO USE MY PENSION AND SOCIAL SECURITY INCOME FOR COST OF CARE IF I AM ON MEDICAID?

Yes. Unless married and your spouse's income is less than MMMNA.

12. WHAT IF I HAVE A HARDSHIP?

The Medicaid rules allow you to create a Special Needs Trust if you must transfer assets for the sole benefit of a disabled person under age 65. Even after moving to a nursing home, if you have a loved one including a friend, who is under 65 and disabled, you can transfer assets into that Trust for their benefit without incurring a transfer penalty. If these Trusts are structured properly, the funds in them will not be considered for Medicaid eligibility.

13. WHAT IS AN INCOME-ONLY TRUST?

If you have an Irrevocable Trust that pays income and you need Medicaid for nursing home costs, the principal in the Irrevocable Trust is not counted for Medicaid, but the income must go to cost of care.

The drawback with using such a trust is that once you put an asset into it, you cannot change your mind and take it out.

14. DO I HAVE TO SPEND DOWN MY ASSETS TO POVERTY?

Applicants for Medicaid and their spouses can protect savings by spending them on non-countable or exempt assets. For example, you can:

- Purchase a prepaid funeral trust
- Pay off your mortgage
- Make repairs or add an addition to your home
- Replace your automobile with a more expensive one
- Update home furnishings
- Pay for more care at home from an agency
- Hire a family member
- You can even buy a new home

In the case of married couples, it is often more important to take any spend-down steps after the unhealthy spouse is in a nursing home, if this would affect the community spouse's resource allowance.[24]

> **Planning Tip:**
> **How to Hire a Family Member**
>
> If you have a child or sibling providing care and you want to pay them, you must do this with a written contract. If you have assets that you want to transfer to your child or sibling, you may be able to do this in the form of compensation.
>
> If, for example, you wanted to give a grandchild money for college, and financial aid in the future wasn't going to be an issue, hire that child and pay him or her for services rendered.
>
> Again, your elder law attorney can advise you.

15. ARE MY ADULT CHILDREN RESPONSIBLE FOR MY MEDICAL BILLS?

Federal law does not permit the states to use the income or resources of non-spouses. States cannot collect reimbursement from these relatives. A few states have laws called filial responsibility laws that make adult children responsible for support of indigent parents. This would only apply for costs not covered by Medicaid.[25]

Beware Filial Responsibility Laws!

Filial responsibility laws vary from state to state. Most agree that children have a duty to provide necessities for parents who cannot do so for themselves. The laws differ from state to state because of legislation and guidelines created by that state's courts, as well as the needs of the adult

---

24 *www.elderlawanswers.com* 2010.

25 Ibid.

child's ability to pay against the needs of the indigent parent.[26]

As of the date of this writing, there were thirty (30) states that have filial responsibility laws and most people have never heard of these laws!

If states opt out of the new healthcare reforms and shift the burden on to the federal government and Medicaid for healthcare, there will be more stress on state budgets. States with filial responsibility laws could turn to those laws to mitigate the loss of federal support for healthcare. Your elder law attorney will have to advise you in this area if you are in a state that has these laws.

16. CAN I BUY AN ANNUITY AND STILL GET MEDICAID?

The Medicaid rules on annuities have changed. Prior to DRA, the answer was "yes." But now it must be a certain kind of an annuity—one that meets Medicaid's rules (irrevocable and non-assignable). It must be an immediate annuity based on the life expectancy of the annuitant with the state as the beneficiary. The exception is if the annuity is in the IRA, then the beneficiary need not be the state.

So why buy an annuity? Well, you convert an asset to income and you might want to take the pressure off a potential recovery against your house. A better way to go is to do a pure grantor trust which a highly-qualified elder law attorney can help you with. Or if you had bought long-term care insurance, or better yet, partnership long-term care insurance. If you are healthy and have the assets to buy the annuity, then using the Partnership LTCi may be a good way to go because then you can protect assets from Medicaid.

17. WHEN IT COMES TO INCOME, WHO IS REALLY COVERED BY MEDICAID?

The answer to this question depends on the rules in your state.

---

26 *The New Old Age* by Jane Gross.

Confused?

The rules are so confusing they create a hopeless web in the different states, requiring that you seek out the advice of a qualified elder law attorney in your state to deal with your state's rules.

Do not be discouraged. Seek out proper help. No one needs to lose everything!

In the next chapter, we will discuss how the VA can help pay for the cost of care in or out of the home if you or your loved one is a wartime veteran, the spouse of a living veteran, or the surviving spouse of a deceased veteran.

CHAPTER FOUR

THE BEST-KEPT SECRET IN LONG-TERM CARE

"Theirs is not to make reply,
theirs is not to reason why,
theirs but to do or die."

-Lord Tennyson

One of the least-known benefits of the Veterans Administration (VA) is a special monthly pension for wartime veterans known as Aid & Attendance (A&A). What makes this program so interesting is that it is tax-free and it covers medical costs that are not service-connected. In fact, as you will see, you don't even have to be a veteran; you can be the spouse of a veteran.

While referred to as a pension, you do not have to be retired military to receive the benefit. Aid & Attendance is a monthly cash benefit paid by the VA to veterans, spouses of living veterans, or surviving spouses of deceased veterans for unreimbursed medical expenses.

A SPECIAL MONTHLY PENSION FOR WARTIME VETERANS

Aid & Attendance (A&A) is for applicants who need financial help to pay for medical expenses in home care, assisted living, board and care, or even a nursing home. If you are a veteran (or spouse) who meets the qualifying conditions and you require help with eating, bathing, undressing, toileting, or any general care, medical, or nursing service, then you may qualify for A&A. Medical care is considered skilled, such as wound care, IV therapy, etc., while nursing services include anything of a personal nature; e.g., help with Activities of Daily Living (ADLs), and it even includes money to pay for medicines and health insurance. In a nutshell, care is any unreimbursed medical care. It also provides payment for individuals who are blind or have a mental or physical incapacity.

Who is eligible for VA pension and A&A?

Aid & Attendance is a benefit paid to veterans or the surviving spouse of a veteran, who have met the asset and income guidelines and who are at least 65-years-old, or if under 65, are permanently or completely disabled and have unreimbursed medical expenses. Benefits for a surviving spouse of a veteran are paid to the surviving spouse if he or she was married to the veteran at the Veteran's date of death and has not remarried a non-Veteran. The VA considers only marriage to opposite sex as legally married.

If you are a **transgender** person who is legally married to the opposite sex, you will need a new birth certificate. Your marriage will need to be recognized in your state for the VA to provide benefits. If you have further questions or want to know how to get a new birth certificate in your state, please contact NCLR (NCLRights.org). This may not have been tested yet with the VA as of the date of this book.

Is this a service-related disability?

A&A need not be a service-related disability. Unlike Medicaid, A&A is not needs-based; it is based on whether UME (unreimbursed medical expense) caused wartime veterans or their spouses to have income below certain levels. It can be, for example, for Alzheimer's disease, Parkinson's disease, etc.

What are service requirements for A&A?

A veteran, a veteran's spouse, or a veteran's surviving spouse may be eligible if the veteran:

◎ Served at least 90 days of active duty (*need not be all at the same time*), one day of which was during a qualifying wartime period, the Veteran did not have to be in combat or overseas; and

◎ Served one day during one of the following periods:

World War II: December 7, 1941 to December 31, 1946
Korean War: June 27, 1950 to January 31, 1955
<u>6 months of active duty are required of vVietnam Vets:</u>
Vietnam War: August 5, 1964 to May 7, 1975
February 28, 1961- if served in Republic of Vietnam only
<u>2 years of active duty is required of Gulf War Vets:</u>
Persian Gulf War: August 2, 1990 to [date not yet determined]
Granada and Panama may count

Was discharged from a branch of the United States Armed Services including the Merchant Marines and Coast Guard under conditions that were not dishonorable. Appendix F provides other services that are covered.

What if my income is too high?

The VA will pay benefits to the eligible beneficiary up to the Maximum Annual Pension Rate (MAPR). Many veterans have high incomes. If your UME (unreimbursed medical expenses) reduces your income below certain levels, you will qualify for A&A.

You can reduce your income amount by deducting all unreimbursed expenses relating to your medical needs. So, regardless of your actual income when you factor in all unreimbursed medical expenses, you might qualify. Unreimbursed medical expenses can include items such as doctor fees, dentist fees, prescription glasses, Medicare premium and co-payments, prescription drugs, health insurance premiums, transportation expenses to physicians' offices, therapy, etc. You can also include payments for personal care, caregiver cost, hiring family as caregivers (with a contract or agreement for services), board and care, and more. Expenses must be recurring to calculate the ongoing monthly benefit.

The biggest unreimbursed expense that can reduce countable income is the cost of home health care, assisted living facilities, or skilled nursing homes.

What is countable income?

Income you receive, including Social Security, employment earnings, pensions, interest, dividends, disability and long-term care insurance payments, etc. Public assistance such as SSI is not counted. If you have a partner who is living with you in a non-married relationship, is not a dependent and has income, don't count that, because you are single to the VA.

Table I-1
Aid and Attendance
Maximum Annual Pension Rate (MAPR)
(2011 Rates)

Status	Monthly MAPR
Single Veteran	$1,644
Veteran with Spouse/Dependent	$1,949
Two Veterans Married to Each Other and Rated A&A	$2,582
Surviving Spouse	$1,056
Surviving Spouse with One Dependent	$1,260
Healthy Veteran, III Spouse	$1,291

What about my assets?

You will be disqualified from A&A if your assets are deemed to be sufficient to provide for your care. There is no set asset dollar limit. The question of whether you have enough assets and will therefore be disqualified is based on your age and whether you are married, single, or widowed. While one may appear to have too much assets to qualify, a properly trained attorney can legally get you to the qualifying limits with the use of proper trusts.

Are there exempt assets?

Certain assets are not included when calculating the amount of assets for eligibility purposes. These assets include your home, a car, and your personal belongings. You need not include these items when determining the amount of assets for eligibility.

What if I have too many assets?

Unlike Medicaid, there is no look-back period. Assets may be repositioned into irrevocable grantor trust (IGT) and held in their current form or converted to income producing assets such as short term annuities to create income, which can then be offset by unreimbursed medical expenses to bring you to the qualifying income level.

You must, however, be cautious, because qualifying for A&A may require planning that will make you ineligible from receiving Medicaid benefits should you need them. A properly trained attorney can advise you about both and help you select the best benefit to pursue.

What if I need Medicaid?

Another important factor that you must consider when thinking about trying to become A&A eligible is that giving away cash or other assets of value can make you ineligible if you need to apply for Medicaid. The rules for VA Benefits and Medicaid are very different.

In many situations Medicaid and A&A can work hand-in-hand and you may qualify for both benefits. In other circumstances, planning for A&A may disqualify you from qualifying for Medicaid. In most states, there is no harm since Medicaid does not traditionally pay for care in your home or in an assisted living facility. The problem occurs when you can no longer live at home or in an assisted living facility and must move to a nursing home.

It is essential that if you are facing a long-term care need, you seek capable legal advice from an attorney accredited by the VA who is skilled in the areas of estate planning, financial planning options, Medicaid, Medicare, income tax, and gift tax, as well as having experience regarding VA rules.

Who can help me apply for A&A?

You or a family member may apply to the VA directly or a qualified service organization may apply on your behalf. The only people who can apply on your behalf are listed as follows:

◉ An attorney licensed to practice law in your state and who is a VA accredited attorney or who works with someone who is VA accredited

◉ A veterans' service organization such as VFW, American Legion, AMVETS, etc.

◎ A state or county official of the Department of Veterans Affairs in your state

◎ A VA accredited private agent

Applying for A&A is very technical and many are denied for lack of providing sufficient information. In addition, if you do not meet the eligibility criteria, those helping you with the application generally do not have the knowledge to get you gratifying results. A qualified accredited estate planning or elder law attorney will have the ability to get you legally to the qualifying limits and insure your benefits are preserved.

How much will this cost?

Nothing! That's correct.

As an accredited provider assisting with A&A benefits, the VA prohibits any fee being charged for assistance in the application process. Attorneys may charge for any legal work needed to get you to the qualifying levels, but not for the application. You can also be charged for an appeal of an unfavorable decision if you decide to pursue it.

What about Susan?

Robert was a Vietnam veteran who served during a qualifying period. Susan, his widow, may be eligible for the VA's Special Monthly Aid and Attendance Pension. She could get up to $1,056 per month tax-free if she qualifies and completes the appliation process properly with the right help.

> ## Meet Sam
>
> Sam is a veteran and his wife has been diagnosed with dementia. They own their own home valued at $150,000, have $20,000 in money markets, and a stock portfolio worth $100,000. Their combined monthly pension benefits and Social Security total $2,500. Sam is finding it difficult to care for his wife, so he has hired a care agency to come in two to three hours a day to assist him with his wife's needs (cost is $2,000 per month).
>
> Sam's unreimbursed medical expenses reduce his income below acceptable limits, but his assets are likely too excessive to qualify. Simple repositioning of Sam's assets with the assistance of a qualified attorney can make Sam eligible for A&A benefits in as little as 30 days.
>
> Do not, however, do this yourself, as you can disqualify yourself from Medicaid by making changes to qualify for VA benefits. Medicaid rules are not compatible with VA rules. This is very technical and must be done with qualified legal help.

As more and more veterans come into the system and need help with care, costs will increase, if not soar. The VA has started to look at transfers and estate recovery at the time of this writing. Administration of your benefit decision can vary from administrator to administrator. It is essential that when it comes to this type of planning, you work with a knowledgeable estate planner or elder law attorney who is also accredited through the VA or works with someone who is VA accredited.

CHAPTER FIVE

WHAT ABOUT INSURANCE? LONG-TERM CARE INSURANCE CHOICES

"You don't need to pray to God any more when there are storms in the sky, but you do have to be insured."

- Bertolt T. Brecht

Long-term care insurance is the only form of insurance that will pay for the cost of long-term care. If you have the health and the time to plan ahead, then long-term care insurance must be considered.

Long-term care (LTC) insurance will pay benefits if you are unable to perform a specified number of activities-of-daily living (ADLs) such as bathing, dressing, eating, etc., or when you have cognitive impairment or dementia caused by Alzheimer's disease or another condition.

Do you have it? If not, why not? If you do have it, do you have enough? Long-term care insurance is part of your long-term care protection plan. It provides cash flow when you are struck with a sudden increase of an additional $6,000-$10,000 or more per month in your cost-of-living. Please see Appendix A for the cost of care in different American cities (2010).

There are a number of reasons people give for not having long-term care insurance. The most common ones are:

◎ Too expensive
◎ I don't need it, i.e., it won't happen to me.
◎ My daughter will take care of me.
◎ The government will pay.

And the newest surprise:

⊚ My husband will care for me.

There are other reasons: It's a waste or money, If I never use it, I've lost all that money. I can't qualify. We will address all of these reasons. But the bottom line is that it is still the only form of insurance that will pay for long-term care expense, whether in your own home, or in an assisted living facility or nursing home.

1. IT'S TOO EXPENSIVE!

Before you say it's too expensive, or what if I pay for it and never use it and skip this section, let's get real for a moment. You need to ask yourself one question. **Insurance is too expensive as compared to what?**

If you can afford to spend $6,000 to $20,000 per month ($72,000-$240,000 per year) today in after-tax dollar costs for an extended period then, by all means, skip this chapter. But if you fall into the category where having an insurance company provide benefits for you to be able to stay in your own home or avoid losing your lifetime assets, then please read on.

We've seen in Chapter One and Appendix A the cost of the various types of care today. If you Google the **Genworth Cost of Care Survey**, you will see what it costs in your area and what you can expect in the future if costs continue as they seem to be going. A better way to check is to visit a few facilities in your area and find out firsthand what they cost. They love to give tours; it's what the marketing directors do.

2. I DON'T NEED IT!

The chances of you needing long-term care at some point in your life are more significant than you think especially if you are healthy today. You have either a 0 percent chance of needing care or a 100 percent chance of needing care. You either die first or age. If you die first it is obviously 0 percent. If you age long enough, you will eventually lose your mental or physical facilities and so it becomes 100 percent. If you age you need to make sure your financial house is in order and that you have a long-term care plan in place.

Please ask yourself, how many years have you been paying auto insurance and how many times has your car been totally wiped out? How about home owners' insurance? How many times has your house burned down to the ground, the pipes froze, or your house was totally wiped out?

Planning Tip:
What is the Right Age to Start a Long-Term Care Protection Plan?

The corollary statement to "I don't need it" is the statement "I'm too young." What age is too young or too old for Long-Term Care insurance?

Most people think about LTC insurance when they are close to retiring. Premiums are much lower for those in their 40s and 50s than for those over age 65.

Michael J. Fox was 30 years old when he first noticed a twitch in his finger and was subsequently diagnosed with Parkinson's disease. Christopher Reeve was 43 when he had his tragic accident that left him a quadriplegic.

So what is the right age? The right age is as soon as you can get it while you are still healthy.

---

3. MY DAUGHTER WILL TAKE CARE OF ME!

Right! Do you really want your family member to be your caregiver or do you want your family member to manage your care? Long-term care insurance can help keep your family together and reduce the stress of caregiving.

Imagine This

You're lying in bed. You are shaking with Parkinson's or you can't remember your daughter's name. Your daughter's teenagers are arguing. Their father has just stormed out the door. They are living paycheck to paycheck because your daughter had to give up her job to be there for you.

It's snowing. The dog is barking. The cat is whining for food. Is this the environment where you will receive the best care?

Families break up, marriages are destroyed, or siblings go to war with each other when a loved one has Alzheimer's disease and moves in. When you think this through, you will realize this is not a realistic option.

If you had the money, you could hire qualified care and manage it. Stress kills 50 percent of caregivers before their recipient. Long-term care insurance provides the money. If you have the health and can qualify for long-term care insurance, then this is a better way to go.

4. THE GOVERNMENT WILL PAY.

In many cases there is no planning or you make irrevocable mistakes that could have been avoided, leaving you impoverished before the government pays. As we've seen in Chapters Two and Three, the price is very high if the government is to pay. Fortunately, as we will discuss shortly, the government offers you tax incentives to use long-term care insurance.

The state's ability to pay may be shrinking as stated in the New York Times headline article of January 29, 2011: "For governors of Both Parties, Medicaid Looks Ripe to Slash." The tighter money gets as more people age, the harder it will be for the government to pay. We discussed the implications of the government paying in Chapters Two and Three.

5. My Husband Will Care for Me.

In the introduction, we discussed that women are more likely to suffer from Alzheimer's disease or suffer a stroke than men. Men are discovering that they are not prepared to be caregivers. Not only are they not prepared to be a caregiver, but they are angry—angry that they have caregiving duties instead of golf or the good life in their golden years.

Do you want to be cared for by someone who is angry? He thought he was going to spend his investments on retirement or starting over with a new business. Now he may be working beyond when he thought he would retire. Is this the life you wanted?

Elder abuse is showing up because of the new trends in role reversals. Is this the life he wanted? Many men who planned to die first because life expectancy tables and traditional estate planning said he would are finding themselves as caregivers.

Anger does not bode well for loving caregiving. A long-term care insurance policy could easily solve this problem by helping your spouse manage your care rather than being the caregiver.

Plan Alternatives

A comprehensive plan will pay for in-home care, assisted living, or a nursing home. There are numerous different types of long-term care insurance policies available today:

- Traditional LTC Insurance
- Partnership LTC Insurance
- Combination Annuity and LTC Insurance
- Combination Life Insurance and LTC Insurance
- Several non-long-term care insurance strategies

The right one for you will depend on your health, goals, assets, and income. You will need to work with a qualified insurance advisor. Let's look at each one.

Traditional Long-Term Care Insurance (LTCi)

This insurance is based on a maximum daily benefit for a period of time. For example, if you buy a policy that has a benefit of $250 per day for three years, you are buying a pool of money that totals $270,000. If you go on claim and don't use the daily maximum, the unused portion rolls forward until it is used.

These policies should only be purchased with a 5 percent inflation rider or at least some inflation protection. With an inflation protection rider, such as 5 percent, your benefit will increase by that percent every year, depending on the contract. As you will see in the tax benefits section of this chapter, your benefits, as well as the inflation protection rider can be entirely tax-free.

Let's say you are 50 when you purchase an LTC insurance policy, but do not need it until you are 80. You will have $1,093 per day of protection or a pool of money totaling $1,180,044. Does that sound ridiculous? Well, not really if you think about what the cost of care was 20 years ago as compared to today.

> **Planning Tip:**
> **Tax Free Growth**
>
> What does a tax-free inflation rider really mean to you and how does this compare to how you could do in an average investment or annuity?
>
> If you earn, say, 8 percent, by the time you pay taxes and the cost of transactions, you might net 4-5 percent. A 5 percent pure tax-free growth rate that is consistent year after year, is guaranteed and paid out in tax-free dollars is viable and hard to beat.

The table below is based on the 2010 Glenworth Cost of Care Survey for a private room in a nursing home. Using the median cost of care for California and projecting that cost out over 30 years, we see the following increase of possible rise in cost of care. We are using California only because it is a large state with a large population.

Cost of Care Projection[27]

Years	Private Room Nursing Home
Current	$87,000/year
In 10 Years	$142,272/year
In 20 Years	$234,144/year
In 30 Years	$377,496/year

If you Google "Genworth 2010 Cost of Care Survey," you can enter your own region or town and run your own numbers.

Since you don't know what it will cost you when you need it, purchasing a policy with a 5 percent inflation rider is not only realistic, but it is a very important component of your long-term care plan. Some agents will recommend that you use a Guaranteed Purchase Option as an inflation hedge because it is less expensive than an inflation rider. The problem with this approach is that you must purchase more insurance every time the option is offered. What if you forget, postpone, or just skip the offer a few times because you realize the price is going up because you are getting

---

27 Based on Genworth 2010 Cost of Care Survey Projections for a median cost of care in California.

older? An inflation rider, on the other hand, is built-in and automatically increases your coverage every year.

Long-term care policies have a waiting period before the benefit starts called an elimination period, which is like your deductible on other insurance. The longer the elimination period, the lower the cost. The cost or premium is based on age and benefits (amount of coverage, length of payments, features, etc.).

Table II-1 illustrates an average cost of a policy in California with a 90-day elimination period, with a $7,500 per month benefit for three years using standard rates. Table II-2 shows the same $7,500 benefit with a 90-day waiting period but for six years instead of three. The reason you might want to consider a longer period is that if you run out of benefits you can turn to Medicaid. Medicaid, as we saw in Chapter Three, has a 5-year look-back period. If you coordinate your long-term care planning properly, you can use Medicaid to create a lifetime benefit as a way to extend your protection. The extra year provides a buffer that you will need to get past denial issues and paper processing time when dealing with your state's Medicaid agency.

If you are in excellent health, married, or live with someone, your rates may be less. Please notice the trend—as you get older, the deposit or premium goes up. The fallacy in waiting is that you may not save money by waiting and you may become uninsurable in the process.

The older you are, the more likely you will have a health history that could work against you or disqualify you. You must qualify for LTC insurance. The saying in the industry is that "you pay for long-term care insurance with money but you buy it with your health."

Table 11-1
LTCi Cost Benefit Analysis[28] [29]

Age	Monthly Deposit	Initial Monthly Pool	Tax-Free Pool of Money Based on 3-Year Duration		
			In 10 Years	In 20 Years	In 30 Years
40	$227	$7,500	$442,800	$723,600	$1,180,440
50	$258	$7,500	$442,800	$723,600	$1,180,440
60	$356	$7,500	$442,800	$723,600	$1,180,440

Table 11-2
LTCi Cost Benefit Analysis[30] [31]

Age	Monthly Deposit	Initial Monthly Pool	Tax-Free Pool of Money Based on 6 -Year Duration		
			In 10 Years	In 20 Years	In 30 Years
40	$351	$7,500.	$885,600	$1,447,200	$2,360,880
50	$461	$7,500.	$885,600	$1,447,200	$2,360,880
60	$560	$7,500.	$885,600	$1,447,200	$2,360,880

28 These rates are based on a single person living alone based on just one company. Many companies will discount rates for two people in a household applying at the same time. Many companies in newer contracts today treat domestic partners similar to married couples. Monthly Benefit $7,500. 90 Day Elimination, 3-Year Plan, 5% Inflation Adjustment

29 The financial calculators and analysis are for illustration purposes only and are projections of hypothetical situations. They are not intended to be financial, tax, or legal advice, nor are they an illustration of any specific product or contract. Calculations from www.ltcia.com.

30 These rates are based on a single person living alone based on just one company. Many companies will discount rates for two people in a household applying at the same time. Many companies in newer contracts today treat domestic partners similar to married couples. Monthly Benefit $7,500. 90 Day Elimination, 6-Year Plan, 5% Inflation Adjustment.

31 The financial calculators and analysis are for illustration purposes only and are projections of hypothetical situations. They are not intended to be financial, tax, or legal advice, nor are they an illustration of any specific product or contract. Calculations from www.ltcia.com.

POOL OF MONEY CONCEPT

The way to think of LTC insurance today is not so much as an amount you purchase per day or month, but as a "pool of money" you can access when you need it and that will roll forward until you use it up. For example, if the daily benefit is $250, and you use only $200, the excess is carried forward. Some contracts treat this as a limit of $7,500 per month, so if you only use $6,000 in a month, the excess rolls forward and extends the contract until it is used up.

A True Story

Maureen, a good friend of the author, speaks of her wheelchair-bound friend, whom we'll call Shirley. Shirley is 85-years-old; she lives in her condo and is immobile except for the wheelchair. Her close friends have passed on and her relatives are all long distance and older. She lives on Social Security, investment, and IRA income. Every day she is thankful she bought a long-term care policy when she was 70, in spite of her friends who said, "It's too late," and "Oh, it's too expensive."

You see, a caregiver comes in every other day to help her around the condo and take her shopping. When Shirley calls, they go out to lunch and have fun. She lives life as best she can in a wheelchair. Shirley says that if it wasn't for the insurance, she would not have the caregiver, be able to go out when she wants to, or even enjoy life.

LTC INSURANCE FEATURES AND BENEFITS

When considering purchasing an LTCi policy, there are certain features you "must have" and there are other features you "should have" depending on your situation.

"MUST HAVE" POLICY BENEFITS

A guaranteed renewable-for-life policy renews automatically unless you stop paying premiums. People who have had their policies a long time are finding that as companies merge, their guaranteed renewable policies continue.

No prior hospital required before benefits are paid.

Planning Tip:
Layering

It is generally never a good idea to replace an old Long-Term Care policy. It is a much better idea to layer a new policy on top of the old policy. In this way, you can increase your benefits, modernize your coverage, and keep the rates from the old policy.

CARE COORDINATOR SERVICES

Your policy should offer the services of a Care Coordinator—a licensed health care professional who can assess your needs, develop an individualized plan of care, and help arrange for long-term care services. There should be no elimination period, which means you have immediate access to a care coordinator.

STAY-AT-HOME BENEFITS

Your policy should provide payment for the following stay-at-home services:

- ◎ Caregiver Training
- ◎ Durable Medical Equipment
- ◎ Home Modifications
- ◎ Medical Alert System

ADULT DAY CARE

This benefit pays for care received in an adult day care center. This benefit is important if the caregiver is working. The adult day care can provide for care while the caregiver is at work.

RESPITE CARE

Your policy should pay the maximum daily benefit for a reduced period of time, such as 31 days per calendar year, for the temporary services of another person or facility to provide care for you. There should be no elimination period for respite care.

HOSPICE CARE

Your policy's nursing facility benefits should be able to cover the expenses incurred for hospice care in any setting when you are not expected to live beyond a certain number of months as stated in the contract. There should be no elimination period for hospice care.

BED RESERVATIONS

Your policy should pay up to 31 days per year to reserve a bed for you in your nursing facility or residential care facility while you are temporarily away.

Planning Tip:
What's a Woman to Do?

You're in an assisted living faculty. You get sick, they send you to a hospital, your stay drags on and on, you're there for several weeks, and it's a really bad trip. Who is paying the bill at the assisted living facility if you are not there?

Suppose it's a nursing home and you go to the hospital. Who pays the bill for your bed at the nursing home? Same problem.

If you are in a facility and have to go to a hospital for a number of days beyond the amount of time the facility will hold your space, you could lose your bed in the facility. The amount of time the bed must be held by the facility is regulated by the state. This Bed Reservation benefit reduces that risk.

INTERNATIONAL TRAVEL

Your policy should pay full benefits in the United States. Anywhere else in the world will depend on what your policy says.

WAIVER OF PREMIUM

No premiums should be due while you are receiving benefits for home care, a residential care facility, or a nursing facility.

TAX-QUALIFIED COVERAGE

Your policy should be tax-qualified so that the benefits you receive are tax-free.

5-YEAR PREMIUM RATE GUARANTEE

Many companies guarantee the premium rates and will not increase them for five years.

OPTIONAL OR "MUST CONSIDER" BENEFITS

The following benefits can generally be added to your long-term care policy at an additional cost. These benefits are optional because all of them may not fit your situation.

SPOUSAL/PARTNER SHARED CARE BENEFIT

Policies that provide this benefit allow you to access your spouse's or partner's benefit if you have exhausted your benefit. Some plans require that there be some benefit left for the spouse/partner, no matter how much you access. Specific terms will be defined in your contract.

WAIVER OF ELIMINATION PERIOD FOR HOME CARE

This benefit allows the policy to waive the elimination period for home care or adult day care. This means that benefits for home care or adult day care begin on the first day of service.

MONTHLY HOME HEALTH CARE BENEFIT OPTION

This option converts your home care daily benefit into a single monthly benefit.

Restoration of Benefits

If you no longer need long-term care services for 180 consecutive days, all benefit amounts paid out will be restored to the original maximum amount in the policy.

Spouse Survivorship and Spouse Waiver of Premium

Under this benefit option, when either you or your spouse receives benefits, the premiums on both policies will be waived.

Limited Payment Option

Under this option, you may pay premiums over the life of your policy or for a limited period of time, after which your policy will be fully paid up. Limited periods of time can include:

- 10 years
- 20 years
- Paid up at age 65

The real benefit of the short-pay period plan is that once the policy is paid up, the company cannot increase your rates even if it has passed the five-year Premium Rate Guarantee previously discussed.

Non-Forfeiture Shortened Benefit Period

Under this optional benefit, your coverage will continue on a reduced basis in the event you stop paying premiums.

Many policies, depending upon your state's law, require an alternative person to be notified if you miss a premium or stop making payments.

Return of Premium

This benefit provides for a refund of premiums paid, less claims paid. Generally, the return of premium is paid upon your death.

TAX TREATMENT OF LONG-TERM CARE INSURANCE

Congress wants you to buy long-term care insurance because they know that the federal government and the states cannot protect you. They hope to inspire you to get the protection you need by giving you tax benefits.

In the following section we are going to see how you can benefit from purchasing LTCi from a tax standpoint.

INDIVIDUALS

Long-term Care Insurance is either Tax-Qualified (TQ) or Non-Tax-Qualified (NTQ). It is very difficult to find a NTQ policy today and most insurance companies don't offer them. A Tax-Qualified policy means that if you are filing a tax return with itemized deductions as opposed to standard deduction, then a portion of the premium is tax deductible.[32] The government imposes a limit on the amount you can deduct called the Eligible Premium, which is adjusted every year for inflation. You are able to deduct the following amounts for a TQ policy in 2011:

Under age 41	$ 340
41 – 50	$ 640
51 – 60	$ 1,270
61 – 70	$ 3,390
Over 70	$ 4,240

---

32 Section 7702(B) of the Internal Revenue Code covers the tax treatment of qualified long-term care insurance.

The amount you can deduct is called Eligible Premium and is the amount you can deduct each year. The older you are, the more you can deduct subject to the 7.5 percent threshold in itemized deductions on your 1040. If you are paying for your spouse, each of you is eligible up to the Eligible Premium Limit.

The deduction goes on Schedule B of the 1040 and is subject to the same rules as your other medical expenses and health insurance premium, which means it must exceed the 7.5 percent threshold to deduct your medical and insurance expenses. This also means that if you are filing a standard deduction without itemizing, you do not have the deduction for long-term care insurance.

More importantly, the benefit from a **TQ policy can NEVER be taxed** if it is paid as a reimbursement for long-term care expenses or is tax-free up to $250 per day for a per-diem policy.

HEALTH SAVINGS ACCOUNT (HSA)

If you have a Health Savings Account (HSA) then you can reimburse yourself for tax-qualified (TQ) Long-Term Care premiums. This means that the premium up to the Eligible Premium would be tax-free even if the HSA is offered through your employer's cafeteria plan.

GIFT TAX EXCLUSION

You can give any number of people $13,000 under the Gift Tax Exclusion Rule of the Internal Revenue Code. You can also purchase LTCi policies for other family members and still maintain the annual gift tax exclusion.

SELF-EMPLOYED (SOLE PROPRIETOR)

A self-employed individual can deduct 100 percent of his or her LTCi premium up to the Eligible Premium Limit without being subject to the 7.5 percent threshold. Any amount over 7.5 percent is not deducible as medical expenses. You can include your spouse and dependents, and it is not necessary to meet the 7.5 percent of Adjusted Gross Income (AGI) threshold.

SUBCHAPTER S, PARTNERSHIPS, AND LLCS

Same tax treatment as self-employed individuals.

C CORPORATIONS

This is where the rubber meets the road and where the government really gives you a tax break. If you are a corporation business owner, you have definite tax advantages. Your corporation is entitled to deduct 100 percent of your LTCi premium as a business expense. There is no 7.5 percent threshold to meet and it is not limited to the age-based Eligible Premium. You can also purchase tax-qualified LTCi policies for select employees without encountering a discrimination issue.

As a C Corporation owner, you have another major benefit. There is no imputed income for the C Corporation when the premium is paid by the corporation for the owner or for the employees.

Planning Tip:
Helping Mom and Dad

Let's suppose that you and your significant other have an incorporated business and your parents are in their 70s.

You can, for example, hire Mom and Dad as directors of your corporation, pay them a nominal salary, and buy LTC insurance for them. You can deduct 100 percent of the premium as a business expense. The catch is they have to do some legitimate work. I'm sure they would love to go to board meetings and "tell" you how to run your business.

This is especially effective if you are a professional or high-earner looking for deductions because to you it is a 100 percent deduction as a business expense, but to Mom and Dad, they can only deduct it if it is over the 7.5 percent threshold. If your parents are retired, they probably can't meet the 7.5 percent threshold on their own. You can substitute your adult children, siblings, or anyone for Mom and Dad.

Planning Tip:
A C Corporation Tax Reduction strategy

Let's say business is booming and you are looking for ways to reduce taxes. You can not only deduct the premium for your LTC insurance for you, your parents, spouse/partner or any-one of your choosing who is a legitimate employee but you pay the premium over a reduced period such as 10 years. This will "fatten" the premium and increase the deduction. You can also add the "return of Premium" Rider. This will return the premium to you estate at your death, tax free.

So, what have you accomplished? You've taken tax

deductible dollars and gotten them back tax-free. If you love this strategy you must clear it with your tax advisor before implementing. Laws change. The government needs money. The rules may be different by the time you read this or decide to act on it. Your tax- advisor will know.

CLASS ACT

In 2010 President Obama signed in the law a health reform bill known as the Affordable Care Act. In the law is the Community Living Assistance and Support Act or the CLASS Act. The purpose of this act is to provide money for long-term care. It was hailed as a fabulous benefit. Its real benefit is the recognition that there are people who don't prepare for the cost of long-term care, or who will procrastinate in obtaining the protection they need until it is too late, or who cannot get it because they have a past or current medical condition. It also has a special provision for people earning less than the federal poverty limit or who are full-time students under the age of 22. Low income earners and students like everyone else, must be at least 18 years old and employed full-time. It also recognizes that if there is a real problem as we age, we may need long-term care and that it is very expensive.

Before you get too excited, let's look at the key provisions.

◎ You have to be an employee to get this benefit.

◎ You have to pay into the program for five years so there is a five-year vesting period.

◎ Your employer has to provide this plan unless your employer opts out of the program.

◎ The projected benefit is $50 per day or inflation adjusted $50 per day.

◎ As of this writing, no one knows when the program will actually start, but it may be in 2013.

Here's the first rub. The cost of care at the time the law passed was approximately $200 per day or more depending on where you were receiving the care. If you study any of the major websites that provide the cost of care around the country, such as the Genworth Cost of Care Survey, or if you talk to care facilities in your area, you will see that there is a mismatch here. While $1,500 per month is helpful, unless you have other resources, how will your CLASS Act policy pay for a cost of care that could be significantly higher?

Here's the second rub. This is a government program. The Department of Health and Human Services could change its mind, discover it's too costly, or make entry restrictive. Medicaid, as you saw in Chapters Two and Three, was originally for the poor and relatively easy to get into. Now it is very difficult to get into and has income and asset requirements. As more people discover they need help paying for long-term care, what other restrictions will the government impose on you when you need it? Also, if an insurance company doesn't meet its contractual obligations, you can sue them. You can't sue the federal government if the Department of Health and Humans Services ends or changes a program.[33]

The CLASS Act will not solve the nation's long-term care problems and it will NOT provide benefits for all of your long-term care costs.[34]

What the government is really saying is that YOU have to prepare for this and that it is your responsibility to do so.

---

33 As the courts challenge ObamaCare and the Congress revisits it, no really knows what the CLASS Act will actually look like as of this writing.

34 *www.cahealthadvocates.org/.../*class-faq.html; 2010 CaliforniaHealthAdvocates.

PARTNERSHIP FOR LONG-TERM CARE INSURANCE (PLTCI)

The Partnership for Long-Term Care Insurance PROTECTS assets from Medicaid spend-down. If you run out of benefits, the amount of coverage you have used protects an equal amount of assets from Medicaid spend-down. If you run out of coverage with traditional LTCi, you then have to spend down your assets before you can go on Medicaid.

The Deficit Reduction Act of 2005, also known as DRA of 2005, defined a new program called the National Partnership for Long-Term Care Insurance. It said that states offering long-term care insurance with the benefits listed below are automatically grandfathered partnership plans with asset protection.

1. Tax qualified

2. Inflation protection for people under age 61

3. Inflation protection—simple or compound for ages 62 – 75

4. Must offer inflation protection to people 75 and older, with the right to refuse.

As of this writing, 35 states have the national plan and four states have the original partnership plan.

Planning Tip:
How Much Partnership Insurance Should You Buy?

When purchasing LTC insurance, there are six critical areas to consider:

1. Type of insurance (Nursing Home Facility vs. Comprehensive)

2. Daily Benefit

3. Duration of coverage

4. Elimination Period

5. Inflation

---

6. Non-Forfeiture features

When purchasing Partnership, however, there are only two real considerations: **daily amount** and **duration**, or length of coverage.

You want to buy enough coverage to protect your Non-Exempt or Countable assets listed in Chapter Three: Understanding Medicaid. So, if you have $325,000 in countable assets that you want to protect, you might buy $300 per day for three years. If you have $500,000 in countable assets you want to protect, you might buy more coverage. If you run out of benefits and have not protected your countable assets, you have to spend down those assets before Medicaid starts paying.

The question you will need to answer for yourself is "How much Non-Exempt Assets do I want to protect?"

Planning Tip:
The Original Partnership Plan vs. the National Partnership Plan

There are two versions of the Partnership plan: the one adopted by the initial four states to have the Partnership program (CA, CT, IN, and NY) and the National plan, which the other 35 states have. The major difference is that in CA, CT, IN, and NY the plan only protects assets against Medicaid spend-down in those states. There is no reciprocity if you move to another state, but benefits do continue. So, if you have a plan from one of these states, it will still pay for long-term care expenses, but it will not protect you against Medicaid spend-down if you move.

On the other hand, the National plan adopted by the other states has reciprocity. So if you move from one of the 35 states after you bought the Partnership plan in that state to another state in the 35-state group, your protection moves with you. Your protection against Medicaid spend-down and your benefits move with you.

insurance carriers and the individual state that has approved it. (See Appendix E for the list of states with the National Partnership Plan.) Your broker must not only be licensed to sell long-term care insurance, but must also be licensed to sell the Partnership LTCi in your state and take additional CEU courses every two years. One of the reasons people don't hear about this is because many insurance brokers are not Partnership-certified. Brokers who are both LTCi-licensed and Partnership-certified have made a commitment to be in the long-term care insurance business.

Partnership LTCi costs the same as traditional LTCi. Partnership plan guidelines, such as an inflation rider or minimum protection amounts, may push you into more expensive plans that cost more than traditional plans.

Planning Tip:
When Mom Doesn't Have Enough Money to Pay for Insurance

Let's suppose that Barbara's total assets are her $200,000 condo and $40,000 in the bank—clearly not enough to pay for long-term care for an extended period of time. Let's also suppose she wants to give all of her assets to her children, both of whom are working. What should she do?

Barbara can buy a Partnership for Long-Term Care Policy equal to the amount of her assets and ask her children to pay the monthly premium. This way they won't have to care for Mom, and if she runs out of LTC insurance, she can go on Medicaid and her assets will be saved for the children even if she runs out of benefits.

If Barbara doesn't buy a Partnership plan, her children can buy traditional long-term care insurance, and if she or they really want to leave a legacy, they can buy a life insurance policy on her. She will have to qualify for the insurance, be open-minded and willing to talk to her children and ask for help. She will have to let the children know that they have a choice—be the caregiver or the care manager and let the insurance help pay for the care.

ASSET-BASED LONG-TERM CARE INSURANCE

The Pension Protection Act of 2006, enacted in 2010, enables you to take payments from annuities or life insurance during your lifetime on a tax-free basis to pay for long-term care expenses. It also allows you to take income that would be taxable from an annuity that is not in a retirement plan and, if you use it to pay for long-term care premium, the income will be tax-free.

COMBINATION ANNUITY AND LONG-TERM CARE INSURANCE

In this type of insurance, you purchase a fixed annuity with a long-term care rider. The amount of dollars you invest is divided by a factor to give you the daily benefit. The company guarantees a number of years of benefit. One national company, licensed in some states, divides the amount you invest by 730 to give you the daily benefit and then multiples the result by 30 to give you the monthly benefit. With that company you pay for two years of benefit but they guarantee six years of benefit. Other companies calculate the benefits differently.

Qualifying for this type of insurance is less stringent than with traditional LTCi or Partnership. The LTCi benefit is tax-free. This strategy works best for non-IRA assets, as there are income tax consequences that must be considered if the funds are in an IRA. Annuities contain limitations, including withdrawal charges, cap rates, fees, and market-value adjustment, which may affect contract values. Guarantees are based upon the claims-paying ability of the insurance company issuing the annuity. You will want to discuss this option with a qualified life insurance specialist.

Planning Tip:
Converting Taxable Annuities to Tax-Free Long-Term Care Benefits

Many people have idle annuities. These are annuities that were bought with the intention of protecting assets and then converting them to income at some point that just never happened. An idle annuity can be a good candidate for a tax-free exchange, also known as a 1035 exchange, to an annuity with a long-term care rider.

Other people have CDs they are holding for a rainy day. That rainy day may come in the form of a long-term care expense need. Why not put some of the CDs into an annuity that has a long-term care rider? This way they still have access to the principal AND they have long-term care protection.

Or they may take the money that was in the CD with its taxable income and put it into an annuity that is tax-deferred. They can then take out the income they need to pay for a long-term care policy and the income would come out tax-free.

You cannot do this with a CD, as the interest would be taxable. Using the annuity strategy, you get previously taxable interest income off your tax return. And, if you follow the rules outlined in the tax treatment section, you might even get income tax deductions for some or all of the premium. Tax-free income becoming tax deductions is not bad. Before you do this, you should review it with your tax advisor.

COMBINATION LIFE INSURANCE AND LONG-TERM CARE INSURANCE

Some life insurance policies have a long-term care feature. Basically, you buy a life insurance policy with a long-term care rider. If you need long-term care, these policies will then pay a percentage of the death benefit every month for long-term care for a pre-set number of years.

You must qualify for the life insurance as well as the LTCi component. The benefit of this approach is that if you die without using all or part of the LTCi benefit, the life insurance proceeds will go to your heirs. Unlike the annuity, there could be more proceeds at death.

The problem with long-term care insurance is that most seniors don't have it when they need it. Why don't they have it? They thought they would never need it and/or they thought it was too expensive. It's expensive when you look at it out of context. When you consider the real cost of long-term care and the fact that you could become impoverished paying for care out of your pocket, it really is relatively inexpensive.

There is still another way that may work for you.

LIFE SETTLEMENT – If you have a life insurance policy that you no longer need because your employer bought it for you, or you bought it for a business need and now that you've retired, you own it but don't want to pay the premium, you have an alternative. Or you might have purchased insurance to protect your spouse and you are now divorced or he has passed away. What do you do with your insurance policy that you no longer want? You can sell it in a process called Life Settlement.

Or, if you are totally averse to long-term care insurance because, no matter what, you won't buy it, an alternative is to buy a large life insurance policy and sell it in the future in the life settlement process. The proceeds from the life settlement can be used to pay for your long-term care expenses.

When you sell a policy through a life settlement, you are selling the death benefit to someone or to a firm that sees your policy as an investment. They will pay you, based on your life expectancy, an amount less than the face amount, but generally more than the cash value.

A qualified insurance broker licensed to sell life settlements in your state can walk you through the process, but generally you need to be at least in your 70s. The older you are, the better. Your tax advisor will need to advise you on the tax consequences.

Planning Tip:
What to do if You Are Uninsurable?

What if I'm uninsurable and can't get either the annuity with the long-term care rider or life insurance with a long-term care rider? Fear not, there is another strategy.

You can get an annuity with an enhanced income option. These are annuities that have a payment option that, should you go to a nursing home, the amount of the payment increases. This is not the same as a long-term care rider because the payment is based on the value of the account times a pre-stated rate that is in the insurance contract.

In plans with the enhanced feature, the amount increases if you go to a nursing home, generally after being there for a period of time. It will depend on the company and its features, but it is a way of creating an income stream for nursing home costs without insurance underwriting.

Frequently Asked Questions

1. What is the best LTC insurance policy for me?

What's best for one person may not be best for another. The benefits and amount of coverage you need depend on your unique circumstances. The needs of a single widowed woman are quite different than a married man, particularly if their economic circumstances are different. Since you are more likely to live longer than a man and more likely to live alone at the end of your life, your LTC insurance needs are different.

2. If I move to another state after buying an LTC policy, will I still be covered?

The answer is generally yes. However, you may want to review your policy with a local agent or broker, as definitions can be different in the new state.

3. Do I really need inflation protection?

With the cost of everything going up over time, including the cost of long-term care, a policy with inflation protection is essential if you want to avoid losing buying power in your benefit.

4. Will I be able to stay out of a nursing home if I buy an LTC policy?

Although many insurance brokers speak of LTC insurance as a way to stay out of a nursing home, this may not necessarily be true in your case. An LTC insurance policy might not keep you out of a nursing home if that is the only place that can provide appropriate care. A comprehensive LTC insurance policy should provide for protection in any setting, including care at home, an assisted living facility, or a nursing home. While most people prefer to receive care at home, you may have no choice if your condition requires care in a facility.

5. SHOULD I CANCEL MY LTC POLICY IF I CAN'T AFFORD TO PAY THE PREMIUM?

Before you cancel your insurance, speak to your insurance carrier about changing your benefit reduction options. If you have paid for the insurance for many years, you probably won't want to give up your policy and waste those payments. Instead, you can reduce your benefits and keep some of the coverage.

6. IF MY HUSBAND IS SHOWING SIGNS OF DEMENTIA, CAN I STILL GET AN LTC POLICY FOR HIM?

It is unlikely that an insurance company would issue an LTC policy to someone who is showing signs of cognitive impairment. You buy LTC insurance with money and pay for it with health. Insurance companies have strict health screening tests.

7. CAN I ADD BENEFITS TO THE LTC POLICY I BOUGHT 15 YEARS AGO?

If you are still insurable and can afford an additional premium, you might be able to add benefits to your existing policy or buy a new one. If you are uninsurable and continue to pay your premiums, your policy will continue to stay in effect.

8. MY EMPLOYER IS OFFERING LONG-TERM CARE INSURANCE. SHOULD I BUY IT?

Yes. If your employer is offering it, it is generally a good deal. The premium will probably be lower than what you can buy individually, and the underwriting should be easier. These plans are also portable so that when you leave your employer, you can take your LTC insurance with you.

9. HOW MUCH COVERAGE SHOULD I BUY?

The obvious answer is to buy the amount of coverage that would pay for the cost of long-term care in your area for a period of time. The underlying question here is "how long should that period of time be?" Traditional thinking says that the average stay in a nursing home is two and a half years, but people with Alzheimer's disease can be in a facility for many years beyond that. Other thinking is to buy a longer term policy or a lifetime policy.

The problem with lifetime coverage is that it can be expensive. A better strategy might be to design your long-term care policy on what is known as "short and fat" rather than "tall and skinny." Short and fat means that you buy a policy of relatively short duration with a large daily benefit to create a pool of money. If you don't use the daily benefit or the monthly benefit, it will roll forward and extend your coverage. Tall and skinny means a smaller benefit for a longer period of time.

The amount of coverage you buy is really a pool of money made up of discounted dollars to keep you at home for as long as possible, and to keep you out of the nursing home. You and an experienced long-term care insurance specialist should create a plan that includes your assets as well as your insurance coverage.

Chapter Six

Planning Ahead: Three Families

"Freedom is always and exclusively freedom for the one who thinks differently."

- Rosa Luxemburg

Overview

In this chapter, we are going to look at three planning situations and see how the strategies we discussed in earlier chapters come together.

In **Family One**, we meet Mary, a single mother, age 50, with two children. Mary is uninsurable because she had a stroke when she was 42. Long-term care insurance carriers do not like strokes. Mary wants to protect herself if she needs long-term care so that her children will not have to pay for her care or take care of her should the need arise.

The best strategies in Mary's case will primarily draw on legal solutions, since long-term care insurance is not an option.

In **Family Two**, we meet Lois and Clark. We'll examine what Lois can do to protect herself and her assets since Clark has already been diagnosed with dementia.

In **Family Three**, we meet Jenny, who is not only healthy and athletic; she is also a marathoner and an avid exerciser. In fact, her sister Mary from Family One thinks Jenny lives at the health club. Jenny, like Mary, has the same asset structure, as both inherited their wealth from the same parents. Jenny's goal is to build up her retirement funds, buy a condo in another state in the not-so-distant future, and yes, protect herself from possible long-term care expenses.

In Jenny's case, we're going to focus on the best insurance solution because it gives her the most flexibility and it is available to her.

FAMILY ONE: MARY UNINSURABLE

Mary, our uninsurable friend, earns $100,000 a year, lives on $50,000, and saves the rest after taxes. She has a condominium worth $400,000 with a mortgage of $50,000. She recently inherited $300,000 from her parents. It is held in money markets and CDs.

Condo Net of Mortgage	$350,000
Money Markets & CDs	$300,000
Mary's Net Worth	$650,000

Mary is concerned that if she needs nursing care or goes into a nursing home like her mother, she will lose all of her assets. She does not want her children to pay for her care. Because of her medical history, she does not qualify for long-term care insurance. Does she have other options?

BASIC RULES WITHOUT PLANNING

Mary's concern of losing her assets and the need of long-term care is legitimate. The reality is that if Mary enters a nursing home, she would have to pay for her care until she spent her assets down to only $2,000. At that point, she would be eligible for Medicaid to pay for her care. While these are the hard and fast rules, Medicaid law also provides room for planning, and when properly done, can ensure that some or all of her assets can be protected.

MEDICAID PLANNING

The key goal is to maintain a proper balance between ensuring Mary has access to her assets when healthy, and her desire to preserve her lifetime of assets and family inheritance for her loved ones.

Under the Medicaid laws, Mary's home is exempt up to $500,000 in value. Some states have raised the limit to $750,000. In addition, she can utilize $50,000 of her inheritance to pay off her mortgage without causing any adverse consequence.

While the house is exempt from determining her Medicaid eligibility, Medicaid would have a priority lien (recovery) against it at her death to be reimbursed for all monies paid on her behalf during her life by Medicaid.

In addition, there would be a question of who would maintain the costs on the condo if she were living in a nursing home. Mary wants to preserve her inheritance for her children to make sure that her Mom and Dad's money stays "in the family." She also would like to protect her home, if possible.

TRUST PLANNING APPROACH

In Mary's case, she can elect to transfer her inheritance and her home to an irrevocable trust and retain limited rights. The most important factor when creating an irrevocable trust is that whatever rights Mary retains will be available to creditors, predators, and will be used in calculating her eligibility for Medicaid. For example, if the trust provided Mary had a right to the trust's assets, then Medicaid would include the total value of the assets in determining her eligibility and she would not qualify. If, however, Mary gave up her rights to the asset, and only retained a right to the income from the assets, Medicaid would no longer determine those assets available to her, but would assess an ineligibility period based on the amount of assets transferred.

Typically, a $300,000 transfer would result in Mary being ineligible for Medicaid for up to 60 months after the transfer, but it could also be only a 20-month eligibility period or less, depending on the cost of care and when she entered the nursing home in relation to when she transferred the assets. Since Mary is only 50, it is very likely she would be able to make the transfer and have it all protected prior to her need for a nursing home. The same could be done with the condo while exempt in determining eligibility; it can also be put in an irrevocable trust with her right to live there and sell it, and replace it with another home any time she wanted.

WAIT AND SEE APPROACH

A final option for Mary would be for her to do nothing and wait until a crisis occurred. If a crisis occurred before age 65, she would be able to take all of her assets and put them in supplemental needs trust (SNT) for her behalf. A SNT is a special trust that the government allows disabled individuals to put their assets in for their lifetime benefit without any penalty for transferring to the SNT. This ensures she qualifies for Medicaid immediately and that her money is protected immediately and available for her for the rest of her life to pay for the things Medicaid would not.

The caveat, however, is that upon her death, Medicaid is reimbursed for the monies they expended on her during her lifetime. This will serve Mary's personal needs but will not ensure that the assets will get to her children. A careful balance between Mary's goals and objectives must be monitored and maintained in determining what would be the best course of action for her.

FAMILY TWO: LOIS AND CLARK

Lois and Clark have been married for 55 years. Clark has recently been diagnosed with dementia and is moving into an assisted living facility. They anticipate that he will reside there for two years before needing nursing home care. Lois and Clark's home is worth $900,000 with no mortgage. He has $600,000 in investments in his name and Lois is wondering how to pay for Clark's care before running out of money so she can be protected and maintain her lifestyle. What are their options?

WAIT AND SEE ALTERNATIVE

One alternative is for Lois to do nothing and wait to see if Clark goes to a nursing home. It is likely that their current income, plus the income from their assets, can cover the cost of assisted living with any shortfall being paid for with their assets. This is a risky strategy, however, especially if Clark ends up needing nursing home care.

BUYING TIME ALTERNATIVE

While Clark resides in the assisted living facility, Lois can begin planning. There are special rules for Medicaid recipients who are married to ensure the spouse living in the community does not become impoverished. As a spouse in the community, Lois's home value is exempt in determining Clark's Medicaid eligibility and, if Clark were to pass away, Medicaid would have no right of recovery against Lois's home. If Lois died before Clark, however, the result is very different and the home could be lost to pay for Clark's care. So protecting the home is very important to plan for. While at first glance it appears Clark would not qualify for Medicaid to pay for his care since he has $600,000 worth of assets, Lois does have some options.

First, she can exempt up to $109,540 of the assets as her spousal exemption. In addition, she can pre-pay for her and Clark's funeral, make improvements to her home, even purchase a new car. Assuming these expenditures amount to $200,000, she still has $400,000 of excess assets. Lois can utilize the interest to assist in the cost of the care. Lois can contact a qualified Medicaid Planning attorney to help her undertake asset protection planning to transfer a significant portion of her excess assets to an irrevocable trust to preserve part of the excess while paying through any ineligibility period the transfer creates. This strategy can minimize Lois's loss to $200,000 to pay for Clark's care if Clark entered a nursing home and only half that currently would be at risk if he stays in assisted living. After that time period, Clark would be eligible for Medicaid.

Instead, Lois can elect to take a majority of her $600,000 and place it into an immediate annuity that pays her a monthly amount. Clark would qualify for Medicaid immediately, but Lois would have to give up Clark's monthly Social Security and pension. In addition, if Lois were to fall ill, the entire annuity amount would be at risk and likely lost to her cost of care, and if Lois lived in New York, she would also have to contribute 25 percent of the monthly payment to Clark's care. Each state is different, so you will have to check with a local elder law attorney for your state's rules.

SPOUSAL REFUSAL ALTERNATIVE

A third and more drastic alternative is that Lois can do what is commonly referred to as a "spousal refusal." That is, she could put Clark in a nursing home and sign a declaration that she "refuses to contribute toward his cost of care."

The spousal refusal is drastic because it requires Lois to essentially disown her spouse after 55 years of marriage. While this is merely a legal strategy, the emotional impact on Lois could be significant and should not be underestimated. If Lois did a spousal refusal, it is likely that the state will sue her for support under the state family support laws. Lois's attorney then negotiates with the local Medicaid department for Lois to contribute a portion of his costs of care which are calculated at the Medicaid rate which is 40 to 60 percent less than the standard private pay rate. By utilizing a spousal refusal strategy, the primary benefit is that Lois's contribution for Clark's care would be at a significantly reduced rate because of the benefit of getting the state's rate for paying for his care rather than the private pay rate.

Having to place a loved one into a nursing home is a catastrophic event both personally and emotionally. The additional impact on an individual's lifetime savings and the fear of losing what they spent their whole lifetime building can be excruciating.

Proper planning in advance can ensure for the proper and easy transition of a loved one to a nursing home without the fear of losing a lifetime of assets.

FAMILY THREE: JENNY INSURABLE

Our friend Jenny is in a much better position to use insurance to protect herself and her assets from a long-term care expense than her sister Mary or even Lois and Clark. Jenny can use one of the insurance strategies to create a tax-free funding plan to pay for long-term care. Her best choice is to use a traditional policy with a cash-first feature. The cash-first feature will pay a portion of her benefit as cash with no waiting period once she triggers the benefits in her policy.

Let's look at the other strategies and see why the traditional LTCi approach makes the most sense for her. Since Jenny is 60, the combination annuity and long-term care policy is not the best approach because if she needs to dip into the annuity for funds, she might have a surrender charge depending on when she took the funds out. Since Jenny wants to buy another house, parking her money in the annuity would be counter-productive.[35]

While the combination life insurance and long-term care insurance is a viable approach, Jenny has no real need for life insurance since she wants to give the balance of her estate to her nieces and nephews (Mary's children) when she passes. She has not indicated an interest to do more for her sister or relatives than what she already has.

This leaves us with the Partnership for Long-Term Care Insurance and the Traditional Long-Term Care Insurance policy. Since Jenny lives in California and wants to retire in Santa Fe, a traditional plan with a cash-first feature works best for her. Since she currently lives in California and

---

35 Another thing to keep in mind when it comes to annuities is if you are under 59 □ and make a withdrawal from a non-qualified, i.e., non IRA, annuity, you will have a 10 percent premature penalty. Since annuities are tax deferred, the IRS says, "OK, but you will have to pay penalty for a withdrawal below age 59 □." In that way it is taxed like an IRA. Also, the gain is taxed as ordinary income and not as a capital gain when you withdraw it from the annuity. If, however, you convert the annuity to an annuity with an LTC rider and take the gain out to pay for long- term care expense, it will then come out tax free. You may want to review Chapter Five as this material can be confusing.

wants to move to another state, a California Partnership plan wouldn't transfer the Medicaid spend-down protection as discussed in Chapter Five. Since the Partnership plan doesn't work for her, she is better off with a traditional plan. The cash-first feature allows her to get cash out of the policy as soon as her benefits are triggered without an elimination period (this feature is not available in Partnership plans).

With the insurance strategy, we need to answer the following questions for Jenny:

◎ What is the future value of the policy?

◎ Will the "pool of money" be enough when Jenny may need care and what is the trade-off between the cost of premium over time versus what she would have to invest at a given rate of return to accomplish the same thing with an investment rather than the insurance pool of money?

◎ Can Jenny do better by investing the premium dollars rather than buying insurance?

◎ What would Jenny need to deposit today or pay every year in and invest to equal the insurance pool of money?

The best way we can answer these questions for Jenny is with the analysis in the following tables.

Table III-1 summarizes the assumptions we are making in Jenny's case. Since we don't know how old she will be when she needs care, we'll do the analysis assuming she will need care at 80 or 85 and will use a traditional policy based on the premium for a 60-year-old. We will also assume that the premium is $4,200 paid every year for 20 or 25 years. If Jenny is truly in excellent health, she may get a better rate. We are not going to assume there will be a rate increase at some time, but there may be, since we don't know when or how much it will be.[36]

---

36 Analysis and numbers from LTCi Pool of Money Calculator.

Table III-1
Jenny's Planning Assumptions

Current Age	60	60
Age Care Begins	80	85
Insurance Benefits		
Benefit – Today	$250/day	$250/day
Initial Benefit Duration	3 years	3 years
Annual Policy Inflation Factor	5%	5%
Premium per Year	$4,200	$4,200
Total Outlay to Start of Care	$84,000	$105,000

Table III-2 answers questions 1 and 2: what is the value of the policy and what will the pool of money be when she needs it?[37]

Table III-2
Insurance Pool of Money vs. Premium Outlay

Age Care Begins	80	85
Beginning Pool of Money	$273,750	$273,750
Future Pool of Money at Start of Care[Mark]	$763,263	$974,138
Total Outlay to Start of Care	$250/day	$974,138

---

37 Ibid.

So, which is better, self-funding and doing it yourself in your own investment program or using insurance and creating a tax-free funding strategy as part of your long term care plan? **Table III-3** addresses this issue.[38]

Table III-3
Insurance vs. Investment

Investment vs. Insurance		
Investment after Tax Rate of Return	4%	4%
Age Care Begins	80	85
Investment Accumulation at 4% growth if Jenny invests $4,200 for 20 or 25 years	$250/day	$250/day
Investment Needed to Match Insurance Pool of Money		
Lump Sum Deposit Needed Today*	$321,817	$337,590
Annual Deposit Needed to Match Insurance Pool of Money	$22,769	$20,779

*Amount Jenny would have to deposit today to match the insurance pool of money

The fallacy with the self-funded strategy is that Jenny must attain at least a 4 percent net after-tax rate of return year in and year out until she needs care. If you were Jenny, you would also need to deposit more money every year than you would with an insurance premium to stay even. The 5 percent or inflation factor you choose in your policy, as we discussed in Chapter Five, is automatic, built-in, and guaranteed.

---

38 Ibid.

If Jenny lives in one of the 35 states that has the National Partnership for Long-Term Care insurance program and plans to stay in one of those states, then the Partnership Plan might be a better way for her to go than the Traditional Plan.

CASE STUDIES CONCLUSION

If you are in a situation like Mary or Lois and Clark and cannot get insurance, then the only direction you can go to protect your income and assets from long-term care expenses is to use a legal strategy with a qualified Medicaid and VA knowledgeable elder law attorney. To not plan could leave you at the mercy of your state Medicaid agency's spend-down and recovery rules or leave you with unnecessary expenses and stress.

Planning is about preparing for contingencies that can do great harm to you and your family/ Long-Term Care insurance is the best deal in town unless you have adequate assets and income to pay for your care. If, like Jenny, you can qualify for it, it is the least expensive way to pay for long–term care.

In the next chapter we will address a major hidden problem that no one likes to talk about, but could wipe you or your loved ones out. We will discuss how to identify and prevent elder financial abuse.

CHAPTER SEVEN

PREVENTING ELDER FINANCIAL ABUSE

"It is an equal failing to trust everybody, and to trust nobody."
- English proverb

A s you get older, you need to be aware that seniors are the target of elder financial abuse. You must take precautions in protecting your assets, well-being, records, and money before you become a victim of financial abuse or exploitation at the hands of others.

You say—not me! It won't happen to me—NEVER!

Well, bad news. The sad truth is that it does happen and it happens more often than not. The worst part about elder financial abuse is that most of the time, the abusers are family members, trusted caregivers, or advisors.

In this chapter, we are going to identify how you can spot it and what steps you need to take to prevent it.

Elder financial abuse is a crime. It involves the wrongful taking of money or property, whether through fraud, scams, predatory caretakers, family, or others. An estimated $2.6 billion is stolen annually from elders.[39]

The personal losses associated with abuse can be devastating and can include the loss of independence, homes, life savings, health, dignity, and security. Victims of abuse have been shown to have shorter life expectancies than non-abused older people.[40]

This chapter will help you recognize the red flags of elder financial abuse and help you learn how to protect yourself and those you love.

---

39 PreventElderAbuse.org.
40 Ibid.

WHAT IS ELDER FINANCIAL ABUSE?

Elder financial abuse includes a wide range of conduct:

◎ Taking money or property

◎ Forging an older person's signature

◎ Getting an older person to sign a deed, will, or power of attorney through deception, coercion, or undue influence

◎ Using the older person's property or possessions without permission

◎ Promising lifelong care for money and not following through

◎ Scams that are fraudulent or deceptive

◎ Frauds that use deception, trickery, false pretense, or dishonest acts or statements for financial gain

◎ Telemarketing scams

WHO IS AT RISK?

The following conditions increase an older person's risk of being victimized[41]:

◎ Isolation

◎ Loneliness

◎ Recent losses

◎ Physical or mental disabilities

◎ Memory loss

◎ Inability to make executive decisions or understand their impact

◎ Lack of familiarity with financial matters

◎ Unemployed family members

◎ Family members with substance abuse problems

---

41 *www.preventelderabuse.org*.

WHY ARE THE ELDERLY ATTRACTIVE TARGETS FOR FINANCIAL ABUSE?

⦿ Persons over 50 control over 70 percent of the nation's wealth. Many seniors do not realize the value of their assets.

⦿ The elderly are likely to have disabilities that make them dependent on others for help. These "helpers" may have access to homes and assets.

⦿ The older person may have predictable patterns such as receiving monthly checks.

⦿ People who are severely impaired are less likely to take action against their abusers as a result of illness or embarrassment.

⦿ Abusers may assume that their frail victims will not survive long enough to follow through on legal action.

⦿ Abusers may assume that their victims will not make convincing witnesses.

⦿ Advances in technology have made managing finances more complicated for the elderly and easier for the abuser.[42]

WHAT ARE THE INDICATORS?

There may be clues or signs that your loved one has been abused. Some of the indicators listed below can be explained by other causes. No single indicator should be taken as conclusive proof. Rather, you should look for patterns or clusters of indicators that suggest a problem.

⦿ Unpaid bills, eviction notices, or notices to discontinue utilities

⦿ Withdrawals from bank accounts or investments that the older person cannot explain

⦿ Transfers from investments that the older person cannot explain

⦿ Bank statements and canceled checks no longer going to the older person's home

---

42 Ibid..

◉ New "best friends"

◉ Legal documents that the older person doesn't understand or remember signing.[43]

WHO ARE THE ABUSERS?

The biggest group of perpetrators is family members. Family members who abuse their elderly relatives include sons, daughters, grandchildren, or spouses.

Family members may have substance abuse, gambling, or financial problems. They may stand to inherit assets and feel that they are justified in taking what is "rightfully" theirs. They may fear that you might get sick and use up their "savings," their "inheritance," or their children's education fund. There may be negative relationship issues going back years where they feel entitled to your assets. There may be negative feelings among siblings or other family members who they want to prevent from inheriting your assets.

According to available studies, says Rabbi Bennett Blum, M.D., only five to 20 percent of cases are reported to an authority (Adult Protective Services [APS], law enforcement, district attorneys, general attorneys, etc.). Of reported cases, family members are perpetrators—55 percent of the time. What is often ignored is the fact that **80-95 percent of cases are unreported!** Furthermore, people who are not family members still constitute nearly half of the perpetrators.[44]

---

43 Ibid.
44 Rabbi Bennett Blum 2010 (Financial abuse, diminished capacity, and undue influence evaluations.)
.

UNDUE INFLUENCE

Dr. Bennett Blum, a forensic and geriatric psychiatrist, defines undue influence as follows:

"Undue influence is a legal term that refers to inappropriate or excessive manipulation exerted against a vulnerable person. The "perpetrators" of undue influence misuse a position of trust or power to benefit themselves— or causes they support—at the expense of their victims. Undue influence is found in many types of litigation. Elder abuse, domestic violence, probate or will contests, professional malpractice, psychological torture, war crimes, and many other situations often involve undue influence or similar manipulation strategies."[45]

"An expert in undue influence assessment will know several accepted methods for evaluating undue influence claims and can clarify: 1) how undue influence occurs; 2) how it developed in a specific case; 3) the psychology of undue influence perpetrators; and 4) the impact of undue influence on victims."[46]

"Someone who seems to benefit at the expense of a vulnerable person will often be required to prove that undue influence did not occur. Some of the relationships that automatically raise concerns about undue influence are:

◎ Attorney/client
◎ Clergy/congregant
◎ Conservator or guardian/conservatee or ward
◎ Parent/child
◎ Physician or therapist/patient or client"[47]

Who is susceptible to undue influence? EVERYBODY!

---

45 With permission from Rabbi Bennett Blum, M.D 2010; www.bennettblum.com
46 Ibid.
47 Ibid.

Just because you are vigorous, outspoken, healthy, and on the ball does not mean that when a major illness or cognitive impairment strikes, you won't be susceptible. A person's biological, psychological, and social issues can leave them susceptible to undue influence.

Tips to Help Prevent Undue Influence[48]

1. How Do I Prevent Undue Influence from Occurring?

In addition to the obvious problems resulting from financial abuse, it is often also the gateway to other forms of abuse, and so is particularly important to prevent. One of the best ways to reduce the likelihood of financial abuse is to ensure the elder has independent advisors. Another is to have several people regularly visit. If possible, seek out services from Area Agencies on Aging, senior centers, and religious centers (churches, synagogues, mosques, etc.) so the elder will have frequent visitors.

2. How do I Identify Undue Influence?

If you are concerned that an elder is vulnerable to undue influence, or if you think someone is engaging in undue influence, become familiar with the IDEAL model (available at www.bennettblummd.com). Undue influence may be prevented if at least one of the major criteria is blocked. For example, taking steps to reduce "isolation" (as defined in the model) or "dependence" have been effective in protecting vulnerable adults.

3. How Do I Stop a Large Purchase or Major Estate Plan Change?

If an elder wants to make a large purchase, give a significant donation, change insurance beneficiaries, or change an estate plan (will or trusts), you can help protect his or her wishes by having an appropriate mental

---

48 Printed with permission from Bennett Blum, M.D 2010.

health expert evaluate the elder for mental capacity, vulnerability issues, and undue influence (see "Screening Experts" at www.bennettblummd. com for help choosing the right person). These evaluations are not covered by insurance.

4. WHERE DO I GET LEGAL HELP?

Keep in mind that financial abuse/exploitation of an elder may be a matter for either criminal or civil courts. Consider contacting representatives of both. For criminal matters, you may contact Adult Protective Services, law enforcement, and the district attorney or attorney general's office. The Public Guardian's Office (sometimes called the Public Fiduciary) also has valuable information.

For civil matters, contact an attorney experienced in this particular type of litigation. Your State Bar Association may also be able to provide a list of appropriate attorneys.

5. HOW DO I REDUCE LEGAL FEES?

Elder abuse litigation is often expensive, time-consuming, and emotionally disruptive, so avoid it, if possible. If litigation is not avoidable, speak to your attorney about hiring an appropriate elder abuse expert early in the process. This can save thousands of dollars—even considering the cost for the expert's fees. Experts can help clarify the issues, direct some investigative efforts, and assist attorneys on developing critical deposition questions.

For more information, see "How Experts Can Help" at www. bennettblummd.com.

CHECKLIST

PREVENTING ELDER FINANCIAL ABUSE

The following helpful hints can help protect you and your loved ones from becoming victims of elder financial abuse.[49]

◊ STAY ACTIVE AND ENGAGED WITH OTHERS.

Isolation can lead to loneliness, depression, and vulnerability. You are in charge: remain active, socialize with your family members and friends, and get involved in activities you enjoy.

◊ MONITOR YOUR FINANCIAL AFFAIRS.

Take your time and consult people you trust in making important financial decisions. If you have a trustee, review your financial decisions with them. If you need a trust and don't have one, an elder law attorney can prepare one and recommend a professional trustee. If your trust is old, it may have become stale and out of date, or the trustee may have died or moved. Talk to an elder law attorney now instead of putting it off.

It is often helpful to have another set of eyes review any documents that involve financial decisions and transactions. Check monthly credit card and bank statements. Check bills for accuracy. Only use direct deposit for Social Security and other frequent payments to prevent mail theft. Sign your own checks whenever possible unless your trustee is paying your bills.

◊ STAY ORGANIZED.

Keep your papers and legal documents in a secure location.

---

49 Compiled from the MetLife Mature Market Institute as prepared in collaboration with the National Committee for the Prevention of Elder Abuse and the Center for Gerontology at Virginia Polytechnic Institute and State University.

Review your wills, trusts, power of attorney, and other important papers, including your insurance policies, at least annually to make sure they're still what you want today. Your circumstances and laws may have changed since you last reviewed them. Power of Attorney and Beneficiary designations and changes may need to be updated. Your attorney and professional advisors can assist you.

◊ DISCUSS THE BENEFITS OF APPOINTING A POWER OF ATTORNEY FOR BOTH MEDICAL AND FINANCIAL DECISIONS WITH YOUR ATTORNEY.

Consider someone you know and trust for your medical power of attorney who is an RN or Certified Geriatric Care Manager.

◊ BE CAUTIOUS IN MAKING FINANCIAL DECISIONS.

Be careful when responding to in-person, mail, Internet, or telephone solicitations. Fraudulent solicitors can be very skilled in gaining your trust. Fraud is rampant in this country, especially for your loved ones who are seniors.

◊ DO NOT BE PRESSURED INTO AN IMMEDIATE DECISION.

When a solicitation sounds too good to be true, it probably is. Speak with a family member, a trusted friend, or advisor before sending money or providing personal and financial information.

◊ PROTECT YOUR PASSWORDS.

Protect your passwords for your ATMs, online accounts, bank, and credit cards. Do not share your passwords with others. Do not use the same password for everything. If you feel someone has seen your password, change it and notify the company immediately.

◊ BEWARE OF TELEPHONE SOLICITATIONS.

You are not being rude when you hang up on a solicitor who calls. Consider using an answering machine, voicemail, or caller ID. You can add your name to the National Do Not Call Registry by calling 1.888.382.1222 or registering your phone number(s) at www.donotcall.gov.

◊ BE CAREFUL OF INDIVIDUALS WHO MAY TAKE ADVANTAGE OF YOU.

As we've previously discussed, elder financial abuse is committed by family as well as strangers. Be cautious if someone asks you to change your will, add his or her name to your trust, bank accounts, or titles on your property. If you feel someone is trying to intimidate or isolate you, contact your family or local police.

◊ BE CAUTIOUS IF SOMEONE ASKS TO BORROW MONEY OR SEEKS YOUR ASSISTANCE WITH FINANCIAL PROBLEMS.

You may empathize and want to help, but be careful that this person is not trying to exploit your good nature. Contact your professional advisor and family immediately.

If you are caring for an elderly loved one or a spouse with memory loss, go over this checklist with them regularly. Make sure that they are surrounded with a trustworthy and professional support team and monitor everything.

Planning Tip

Clarinda Cole Lustig, RN, who has supervised the care for an elderly client, recommends keeping close contact with the elderly person and their family. She says that frequent visits and regular short phone calls create trust and a feeling of safety for the elderly person.

Chapter Eight

Summing Up and Getting Assistance

"A journey of a thousand miles begins with a single step."
- Lao-Tzu

Obsessing about long-term care and how to pay for it is bad for your happiness and probably for your health too. As a financial advisor for over 30 years, I've come to strongly believe that the people who take care of the basics and make sure the basics are in place and are current are well ahead of the curve on the path of life.

What does this mean to you? It means having plenty of long-term care insurance, having your legal documents current and in place, having a family care plan with ongoing communication with your loved ones, and everything else we've discussed in this book. But how do you do it? We know much of what we've discussed is not a do-it-yourself program.

There are three groups who can help you:

◉ Geriatric Care Managers
◉ Qualified Financial Advisors
◉ Elder Law Attorneys

Geriatric Care Management

There is a new field called geriatric care management that can help you decide on the most appropriate long-term care for you or a loved one.

A professional Geriatric Care Manager (GCM) may be a social worker, a nurse, a gerontologist, or another human services professional who serves older people and their families. The GCM usually steps in when you or your family is in a crisis.

Geriatric care management is also a preventive, on-demand service that can increase the quality of an older person's life. It can manage all the players rendering services to the older person. It offers assurance and peace of mind to the adult children of the older individual. The GCM's job is similar to the role of case managers and uses all the classic tools of case management, but specializes in serving adults 65 and older by offering a personalized service.[50]

QUALIFIED FINANCIAL ADVISOR

A financial advisor who specializes in working with elder planning issues can be very helpful in both crisis planning and especially pre-planning. The advisor should have at least one of the following designations: CFP, CLU, or ChFC, and have been in the field at least five years. The longer, the better! The advisor you work with should have a working relationship with an elder law attorney and a geriatric care or case manager. The type of questions you would ask are very similar to the questions you would ask an attorney as listed in the following sections.

Questions to ask:

◎ How long have you been in practice?
◎ What licenses do you have and how long have you been licensed?
◎ What state or states are you licensed in? (It must be your state.)
◎ How are you paid?
◎ What areas of financial advisory or insurance do you specialize in?
◎ What percentage of your practice is devoted to retirees and the elderly?
◎ Is there a fee for the first consultation?
◎ What information should I bring to the first meeting?

The answers to these questions will help determine whether this advisor is the right one for you. Asking for references is always a good idea.

---

50 Handbook of Geriatric Care Management, Second Edition, 2007 Page 3, Editor Cathy Jo Cress.

ELDER LAW ATTORNEY

The National Academy of Elder Law Attorneys defines elder law by what the clients' needs are and what areas of legal issues are covered by the attorney. Elder law attorneys focus on the legal needs of the elderly and work with a wide variety of legal tools to meet the goals and objectives of older clients. Under this approach, elder law practitioners handle general estate planning issues and counsel their clients about planning for incapacity with alternative decision-making documents. The attorney assists in planning for long-term care needs including nursing home care, locating appropriate care, and coordinating private and public resources to finance the cost of care.[51]

The areas that are covered by an elder law attorney can include:

- Estate planning
- Probate
- Administration and management of trusts and estates
- Nursing home issues
- Elder abuse and fraud recovery
- Housing issues
- Age discrimination
- Public and private retirement benefits
- Survivor and pension benefits
- Health law
- Mental health law

Most elder law attorneys do not specialize in every one of these areas. So when an attorney says he or she practices elder law, it is your job to find out what areas they work in and how long they have been doing that. Do they work in the field of elder law regularly and consistently, or is this a side activity to a general practice? The following questions will help you identify if this attorney is the right one for you:

---

51 Elder Law and Elder Law Attorney definitions and questions printed with permission from the National Academy of Elder Law Attorneys ©2008

QUESTIONS TO ASK FIRST

◎ How long have you been in practice?

◎ Do you practice in a particular area of law, and what is that?

◎ How long have you been in this field?

◎ What percentage of your practice is devoted to elder law?

◎ Is there a fee for the first consultation and how much is that?

◎ What information should I bring to the first meeting?

The answers to these questions will help you determine whether this particular attorney is one that you would want to meet. If you or a loved one is in a crisis, as we've discussed, you will want to meet with an attorney ASAP. Denial and procrastination could be financially disastrous for you or your loved one. Someone with a cognitive impairment, dementia, or Alzheimer's won't know they need help. It's up to you to take the steps. If you are faced with an immediate Medicaid or VA-related decision, you need to meet an attorney as soon as possible.

QUESTIONS TO ASK ONCE YOU HAVE FOUND AN ATTORNEY

Once you have found an appropriate attorney, make an appointment to see them. You will be asked to give the attorney an overview of the reasons you are seeking assistance. So be sure to organize your financial and legal documents to bring to the appointment. Many times, legal documents are out of date, years old, and needs may have changed. Bring them anyway.

After you have explained your situation, ask:

◎ What will it take to resolve this situation?

◎ Are there alternative courses of action?

◎ What are the advantages and disadvantages of each course of action?

◎ Who will handle my case?

◉ How many similar cases have you handled?

◉ If a trial is involved, who will handle that?

◉ Are you a member of the National Academy of Elder Law Attorneys?

◉ What other organizations do you belong to that focus on elder law?

◉ How are fees calculated?

◉ How much do you think it will cost to resolve my problem, and how long will it take?

FEES

Nobody likes to pay fees. In fact, nobody likes to ask about fees. There are many different ways an attorney can calculate fees. You must ask this in the beginning. You will need to find out how the attorney bills you: Will you pay weekly? Will there be a retainer? Will it be monthly? Will they round up every 15 minutes? Will they round up at all? You need to know because what you want is for there to be no surprises later on. This is stressful enough. And then get it in writing! The writing can be in the form of a letter or formal contract. Even if your agreement remains oral, you have made a contract and are responsible for all charges for work done.

HOW DO YOU FIND AN ELDER LAW ATTORNEY?

There are a number of websites that can refer an elder law attorney. Once you have someone you want to call, follow the procedures listed above, or seek a referral from an attorney you know.

www.medicaidpracticenetwork.com – David Zumpano has an education program and network for attorneys who practice in the field of elder law
www.NAELA.org – National Academy of Elder Law Attorneys
www.ElderLawAnswers.com
www.NELF.org – National Elder Law Foundation
www.CANHR.com – California Association of Nursing Home Reform

And, In Conclusion . . .

Do you remember Smokey the Bear's old saying: "Only you can prevent forest fires"? I'm not sure that's entirely true when it comes to long-term care, but what is true is that you can maximize your options by planning, whether you are planning ahead or in a crisis.

Well, here we are. You have the tools, a guide, and what you need to do to pay for long-term care without going broke. It's really up to you to take the next step. Please let me know how it is going at Harold@HaroldLustig.com.

Smokey the Bear and I are cheering for you.

APPENDIX A
Average Annual Cost of Care in 2010[52]

City	Nursing Home Semi-Private Room	Assisted Living	Home Health Aid
Atlanta, GA	$58,400	$33,000	$42,328
Baltimore, MD	$88,330	$36,000	$46,332
Boston, MA	$110,807	$55,620	$57,200
Charlotte, NC	$67,160	$37,800	$40,040
Chicago, IL	$63,875	$49,920	$49,192
Cleveland, OH	$71,175	$34,200	$43,403
Denver, CO	$74,278	$43,500	$48,620
Dallas, TX	$46,173	$35,970	$41,070
Detroit, MI	$76,650	$39,510	$43,472
Hartford, CT	$128,663	$54,000	$44,616
Honolulu, HI	$105,850	$45,000	$50,336
Kansas City, MO	$53,553	$28,170	$42,053
Las Vegas, NV	$69,350	$30,600	$45,142
Los Angeles, CA	$67,525	$42,000	$44,616
Miami, FL	$80,300	$21,600	$36,608
Milwaukee, WI	$88,454	$42,420	$49,192
Nashville, TN	$60,773	$39,390	$42,328
Manhattan, NY	$159,790	$20,640	$43,472
Orlando, FL	$76,650	$31,206	$40,383
Phoenix, AZ	$64,514	$36,600	$50,313
Pittsburgh, PA	$87,600	$29,250	$45,714
Portland, OR	$80,300	$44,310	$49,192
Rochester, NY	$110,960	$39,060	$48,620
San Diego, CA	$74,825	$39,000	$46,904
San Francisco, CA	$87,600	$45,000	$22,100
Salt Lake City, UT	$58,035	$43,170	$48,048

---

52 Per Genworth Financial: 2010 Cost of Care Survey

Seattle, WA	$85,775	$48,000	$57,772
St. Louis, MO	$48,326	$34,227	$47,934
Washington DC	$81,213	$48,000	$45,760

APPENDIX B
Community Spouse Resource Allowance (CSRA) by State
2011 Costs[53]

State	Community Spouse Resource Allowance	State	Resource Allowance
Alabama	$25,000-109,560	Nebraska	$21,912-109,560
Alaska	$109,560	Nevada	$21,912-109,560
Arizona	$21,912-109,560	New Hamp.	$21,912-109,560
Arkansas	$21,912-109,560	New Jersey	$21,912-109,560
California	$109,560	New Mexico	$31,290-109,560
Colorado	$109,560	New York	$74,820-109,560
Connecticut	$21,912-109,560	N. Carolina	$21,912-109,560
Delaware	$25,000-109,560	N. Dakota	$21,912-109,560
Florida	$21,912-109,560	Ohio	$21,912-109,560
Georgia	$109,560	Oklahoma	$25,000-109,560
Hawaii	$109,560	Oregon	$21,912-109,560
Idaho	$21,912-109,560	PA	$21,912-109,560
Illinois	$109,560	R I	$21,912-109,560
Indiana	$21,912-109,560	S. Carolina	$66,480
Iowa	$24,000-109,560	S. Dakota	$21,912-109,560
Kansas	$21,912-109,560	Tennessee	$21,912-109,560
Kentucky	$21,912-109,560	Texas	$21,912-109,560
Louisiana	$109,560	Utah	$21,912-109,560
Maine	$109,560	Vermont	$109,560
Maryland	$21,912-109,560	Virginia	$21,912-109,560
MA	$109,560	Washington	$48,639-109,560
Michigan	$21,912-109,560	Wash D. C.	$21,912-109,560
Minnesota	$31,094-109,560	W. Virginia	$21,912-109,560
Mississippi	$109,560	Wisconsin	$50,000-109,560
Missouri	$21,912-109,560	Wyoming	$109,560
Montana	$21,912-109,560		

---

53 Federal & state information provided by Elder Planning Law Center, LLC, New Hartford, NY

APPENDIX C
Monthly Minimum Maintenance Needs Allowance (MMMNA) by State For 2011[54]

State	MMMNA	State	MMMNA
Alabama	$1,822	Nebraska	$1,823-2,739
Alaska	$2,739	Nevada	$1,822-2,739
Arizona	$1,822-2,739	New Hamp.	$1,822-2,739
Arkansas	$1822-2,739	New Jersey	$1,822-2,739
California	$2,739	New Mexico	$1,822-2,739
Colorado	$1,822-2,739	New York	$2,739
Connecticut	$1,821-2,739	N. Carolina	$1,822-2,739
Delaware	$1,821-2,739	N. Dakota	$2,267-2,739
Florida	$1,822-2,739	Ohio	$1,821-2,739
Georgia	$2,739	Oklahoma	$2,739
Hawaii	$2,739	Oregon	$1,822-2,739
Idaho	$1,822-2,739	Penn	$1,822-2,739
Illinois	$2,739	R. I.	$1,821-2,739
Indiana	$1,823-2,739	S. Carolina	$2,739
Iowa	$2,739	S. Dakota	$1,821-2,739
Kansas	$1,822-2,739	Tennessee	$1,822-2,739
Kentucky	$1,821-2,739	Texas	$2,739
Louisiana	$2,739	Utah	$1,822-2,739
Maine	$1,822-2,739	Vermont	$1,829-2,739
Maryland	$1,821-2,739	Virginia	$1,822-2,739
Mass	$1,822-2,739	Washington	$1,821-2,739
Michigan	$1,822-2,739	Wash D. C.	$2,739
Minnesota	$1,823-2,739	W. Virginia	$1,822-2,739
Mississippi	$2,739	Wisconsin	$2,428-2,739
Missouri	$1,822-2,739	Wyoming	$2,739
Montana	$1,823-2,739		

---

54 Federal & state information provided by Elder Planning Law Center, LLC, New Hartford, NY

APPENDIX D
Monthly Nursing Home Cost
Used for Calculating Penalty by State for 2011[55]

State	Monthly Nursing Home Care	State	Monthly Nursing Home Care
Alabama	$4,800	Nebraska	Varies
Alaska	Varies- Anchorage: $10,000	Nevada	$5,865
Arizona	$5,135-5,778	New Hampshire	$7,999
Arkansas	$4,514	New Jersey	$7,282
California	$6,311	New Mexico	$5,774
Colorado	$6,267	New York	$7,264 -11,227
Connecticut	$10,366	N. Carolina	$5,500
Delaware	$6,402	N. Dakota	$6,577
Florida	$5,000	Ohio	$6,023
Georgia	$4,917	Oklahoma	$4,041
Hawaii	$8,850	Oregon	$6,494
Idaho	$6,494	Penn	$7,515
Illinois	Monthly Private Pay Rate	R. I.	$7,777
Indiana	$4,826	S. Carolina	$5,380
Iowa	$4,843	S. Dakota	$4,895
Kansas	$4,150	Tennessee	$3,874
Kentucky	$5,385	Texas	$3,981
Louisiana	$4,000	Utah	$4,526
Maine	$7,258	Vermont	$6,633
Maryland	$6,800	Virginia	No.Va: $6,654
Mass	$8,334		Elsewhere: $4,954
Michigan	$6,816	Washington	$6,905
Minnesota	$5,372	Wash D. C.	$7,149
Mississippi	$4,600	W. Virginia	$5,087
Missouri	$3,960	Wisconsin	$6,216
Montana	$5,377	Wyoming	$6,023

---

55 Federal & state information provided by Elder Planning Law Center, LLC, New Hartford, NY

APPENDIX E
States with National Long-Term Care Partnership Program[56]

. . . .

These states have the National Long-Term Care Partnership Program. The original four states, California, Connecticut, Indiana and New York; have partnership plans but do not have reciprocity and are not in this list.

Alabama	New Hampshire
Arizona	New Jersey
Colorado	North Carolina
Delaware	North Dakota
Florida	Ohio
Georgia	Oklahoma
Idaho	Oregon
Iowa	Pennsylvania
Kansas	South Carolina
Kentucky	South Dakota
Louisiana	Tennessee
Maine	Texas
Maryland	Utah
Minnesota	Virginia
Missouri	West Virginia
Montana	Wisconsin
Nebraska	Wyoming
Nevada	

---

56 This list of states is as of this writing. Please check with your insurance broker to find out if the Partnership Program is currently available in your state.

APPENDIX F
Little-Known Groups Qualifying for VA Benefits

· ·

In addition to active duty vets from the armed services, these little-known groups also meet the active duty qualification for VA benefits. If you belonged to any of these groups and received a discharge by the Secretary of Defense, your service meets the active duty service requirement for benefits:

- Recipients of the Medal of Honor
- Women Air Force Service Pilots (WASPs)
- WWI Signal Corps Female Telephone Operators Unit
- WWI Engineer Field Clerks
- Women's Army Auxiliary Corps (WAAC)
- Female clerical employees of the Quartermaster Corps serving with the American Expeditionary Forces in WWI
- Civilian employees of Pacific naval air bases who actively participated in defense of Wake Island during WWII
- Reconstruction aides and dietitians of WWI
- Male civilian ferry pilots
- Wake Island defenders from Guam
- Civilian personnel assigned to OSS secret intelligence
- Guam Combat Patrol
- Quartermaster Corps members of the Keswick crew on Corregidor during WWII
- US civilians who participated in the defense of Bataan
- US merchant seamen who served on block ships in support of Operation Mulberry in the WWII invasion of Normandy
- American merchant marines in oceangoing service during WWII
- Civilian Navy IFF radar technicians who served in combat areas of the Pacific during WWII

◎ US civilians of the American Field Service who served overseas under US armies and US army groups in WWII

◎ US civilian employees of American Airlines who served overseas in contract with the Air Transport Command between 12/14/41 and 8/14/45

◎ Civilian crewmen of certain US Coast and Geodetic Survey vessels between 12/7/41 and 8/15/45

◎ Members of the American Volunteer Group (Flying Tigers) who served between 12/7/41 and 8/14/45

◎ US civilian flight crew and aviation ground support of TWA who served overseas between 12/14/41 and 8/14/45

◎ US civilian flight crew and aviation ground support of Consolidated Vultee Aircraft Corp. who served overseas between 12/14/41 and 8/14/45

◎ Honorably discharged members of the American Volunteer Guard, Eritrea Service Command, between 6/21/42 and 3/31/43

◎ US civilian flight crew and aviation ground support of Northwest Airlines who served overseas between 12/14/41 and 8/14/45

◎ US civilian female employees of the US Army Nurse Corps who served in the defense of Bataan and Corregidor from 1/2/42 to 2/3/45

◎ US civilian flight crew and aviation ground support of Braniff Airways who served overseas in the North Atlantic between 2/26/42 to 8/14/45

◎ Chamorro and Carolina former native police who received military training in the Donnal area of central Saipan and were placed under command of Lt. Casino of the 6th Provisional Military Police Battalion to accompany US Marines on active combat patrol from 8/19/45 to 9/2/45

◎ The operational Analysis Group of the Office of Scientific Research and Development, Office of Emergency Management, which served overseas with the US Army Air Corps from 12/7/41 through 8/15/45

◎ Honorably discharged members of the Alaska Territorial Guard during WWII

APPENDIX G
CAREGIVER RESOURCES

. . . .

These organizations offer information for caregivers. To learn more about support groups, services, research, and additional publications, you may wish to contact the following:

AARP
601 E Street, NW
Washington DC 20049
1-888-687-2277 (toll-free)
www.aarp.org
AARP is a nonprofit organization that advocates for older Americans' health, rights, and life choices. Local chapters provide information and services on crime prevention, consumer protection, and income tax preparation. Members can join group health, auto, life, and home insurance programs, investment plans, or a discount mail-order pharmacy service. The AgeLine database, available on CD-ROM, contains extensive resources on issues of concern to older people. Publications are available on housing, health, exercise, retirement planning, money management, leisure, and travel.

Alliance for Aging Research
2021 K Street, NW, Suite 305
Washington DC 20006
202-293-2856
www.agingresearch.org
The Alliance is a nonprofit citizen advocacy organization offering free publications including Investing in Older Women's Health, Meeting the Medical Needs of the Senior Boom, Delaying the Diseases of Aging, and other aging-related subjects such as menopause, how to age with ease, and health care options under Medicare.

Alzheimer's Association
225 N Michigan Avenue, Floor 17
Chicago, IL 60601

1-800-272-3900 (toll-free)

www.alz.org

The Association is a nonprofit organization offering information and support services to people with Alzheimer's disease (AD) and their families. The Association funds research to find a cure for AD and provides information on caregiving. A free catalog of educational publications is available in English and Spanish. Contact the 24-hour, toll-free telephone line to link with local chapters and community resources.

Alzheimer's Foundation of America (AFA)

322 Eighth Avenue, 7th Floor

New York, NY 10001

1-866-232-8484 (toll-free)

www.alzfdn.org

The AFA is a non-profit foundation comprised of member and associate member organizations across the United States that provide care to individuals affected by Alzheimer's disease and related illnesses. The Foundation's goal is to meet the educational, social, practical, and emotional needs of individuals with the disease and their families and caregivers through its nationwide hotline, support groups, conference, and other hands-on services. Contact AFA's toll-free number to receive a referral to an appropriate community medical and/or support service.

American Association for Geriatric Psychiatry (AAGP)

7910 Woodmont Avenue, Suite 1050

Bethesda, MD 20814-3004

301-654-7850

www.aagpgpa.org

The Association works to improve the mental health and well-being of older people. Contact AAGP for information and referrals to geriatric psychiatry and specialists. Available publications include Growing Older, Growing Wiser; Coping with Expectations, Challenges and Changes in Later Years, and brochures on topics such as Alzheimer's disease, depression, and the role of the geriatric psychiatrist. Some consumer publications are free.

American Association of Homes and Services for the Aging (AAHSA)

2519 Connecticut Avenue, NW

Washington DC 20008-1520

202-783-2242

www.aahsa.org

AAHSA is a national organization with 5,500 nonprofit members that provide older people with in-home services as well as information on adult day services, home health, community services, senior housing, assisted living residences, continuing care retirement communities, and nursing homes.

American Dietetic Association (ADA)

120 South Riverside Plaza, Suite 2000

Chicago, IL 60606-6995

1-800-877-1600 (toll-free)

www.eatright.org

ADA is a professional society of registered dieticians and other dietetic professionals who provide nutrition information, education, counseling, and care. One of ADA's professional practice groups focuses on the special needs of older people and offers nutrition counseling and indirect assistance through state and local meal programs. Call ADA to locate a registered dietician.

American Federation for Aging Research (AFAR)

50 West 39th Street, 16th Floor

New York, NY 10018

212-703-9977; 1-888-582-2327 (toll-free)

www.afar.org; www.infoaging.org

AFAR is a nonprofit organization dedicated to supporting basic aging research. AFAR funds a wide variety of cutting-edge research on the aging process and age-related diseases. Visit the website for a list of free publications. Infoaging.com provides the latest information on the biology of aging, common diseases of aging, and healthy lifestyles.

American Health Assistance Foundation (AHAF)

22512 Gateway Center Drive

Clarksburg, MD 20871

1-800-437-2423 (toll-free); 301-948-3244

www.ahaf.org

The American Health Assistance Foundation (AHAF) is a non-profit organization that funds research seeking cures on Alzheimer's disease, age-related macular degeneration, and glaucoma. AHAF provides the public with information about risk factors, preventive lifestyles, available treatments, and coping strategies toll-free via publications, their website, and Information Services staff.

American Health Care Association (AHCA)

1201 L Street, NW

Washington DC 20005

202-842-4444 or 1-800-321-0343 (toll-free)

www.ahcancal.org

AHCA represents and advocates for the long term care community to government, business leaders, and the general public. AHCA is also the largest association of long term and post-acute care providers that also advocates on a state level through its National Center for Assisted Living (NCAL) division.

American Medical Directors Association (AMDA)

11000 Broken Land Parkway, Suite 400

Columbia, MD 21044

410-740-9743 or 1-800-876-2632 (toll-free)

www.amda.com

AMDA is a professional association of medical directors, physicians, and others practicing in the long-term care continuum and provides education, advocacy, information, and professional development to promote the delivery of quality long-term care medicine. AMDA membership funds long-term care research through its AMDA Foundation. AMDA also provides continuing education and certification to its membership via an e-university program, as well as administrative and management support at the state level via their LTC Direct division.

American Parkinson's Disease Association (APDA)

135 Parkinson Avenue

Staten Island, NY 10305

1-800-223-2732 (toll-free); 718-981-8001

www.apdaparkinson.org

APDA funds research to find a cure for Parkinson's disease. APDA's toll-free line refers callers to local chapters for information on community services, specialists, and treatments. Publications and educational materials are available on Parkinson's disease, speech therapy, exercise, diet, and aids for daily living.

American Physical Therapy Association (APTA)

1111 North Fairfax Street

Alexandria, VA 22314

1-800-999-2782 (toll-free); 703-684-2782

www.apta.org

APTA is an organization of physical therapists providing referrals to APTA geriatric-certified therapists and information on debilitating ailments like arthritis, stroke, scoliosis, and sudden onset of illness. APTA's Section on Geriatrics offers publications on topics such as osteoporosis; incontinence; neck pain; carpal tunnel syndrome; hip, knee, or shoulder care; and what physical therapists can offer older adults.

American Psychiatric Association (APA)

1000 Wilson Boulevard, Suite 1825

Arlington, VA 22209-3901

703-907-7300

www.psych.org

APA is an association of psychiatrists and physicians specializing in diagnosing and treating people with mental and emotional disorders. Its Council on Aging establishes standards for psychiatric care of older people. Contact the APA for information on elder care issues, including medication use by older people, treatment of Alzheimer's disease, and nursing homes. Contact APA for referrals to local psychiatrists.

American Psychological Association (APA)

750 First Street, NE

Washington DC 20002-4242

1-800-374-2721 (toll-free) 202-336-5500

www.apa.org

APA is a professional society of psychologists who provide assistance and information on mental, emotional, and behavioral disorders. Contact the APA for a list of state chapters, information on the psychosocial aspects of aging, and referrals to APA-member psychologists. The APA's Office of Aging produces publications on topics such as dementia and dementia research. Publications include a quarterly subscription magazine, Psychology and Aging.

American Society on Aging (ASA)

833 Market Street, Suite 511

San Francisco, CA 94103

1-800-537-9728 (toll-free) 415-974-9600

www.asaging.org

ASA is a nonprofit organization providing information about medical and social practice, research, and policy pertinent to the health of older people. Membership and subscriptions to Generations, a quarterly journal, and Aging Today, the Society's bimonthly news magazine, are available to the public. A catalog of books for sale and other educational materials are available on the website.

Americans for Better Care of the Dying

1700 Diagonal Road, Suite 635

Alexandria, VA 22314

703-647-8505

www.abcd-caring.org

Americans for Better Care of the Dying is dedicated to improving the care of Americans who are at the end of their lives. ABCD produces a variety of publications. Check the website or call for more information.

ARCH National Respite Network and Resource Center

800 Eastowne Drive, Suite 105

Chapel Hill, NC 27514

919-490-5577

www.archrespite.org

This national resource center provides information on respite care and a respite locator program, technical assistance to state organizations, and an information clearinghouse.

Arthritis Foundation (AF)

PO Box 7669

Atlanta, GA 30357

1-800-283-7800 (toll-free); 404-965-7888; 404-872-7100

www.arthritis.org

AF is a nonprofit organization focused on research and information to cure, prevent, or better treat arthritis and related diseases (such as lupus erythematosus and rheumatism). Local chapters provide free seminars as well as information on specialists and support groups. Publications and videos are available on topics such as self-help and exercise therapy.

Assisted Living Federation of America (ALFA)

1650 King Street, Suite 602

Alexandria, VA 22314

703-894-1805

www.alfa.org

ALFA represents for-profit and nonprofit providers of assisted living, continuing-care retirement communities, independent living, and other forms of housing and services. The Federation works to advance the assisted living industry and enhance the quality of life for consumers.

B'nai B'rith

2020 K Street, NW 7th Floor

Washington DC 20006

www.bnaibrith.org

B'nai B'rith is the world's oldest and largest Jewish service organization, providing community service, education, and advocacy. Its Center for Senior Housing and Services sponsors housing and travel for senior citizens. A list of publications is available.

BenefitsCheckUp

www.benefitscheckup.org

A free online service provided by the National Council on Aging that screens for benefits programs for seniors with limited income and resources that can help them meet health care costs.

Best of the Web Senior Housing Directory

seniorhousing.botw.org

The Best of the Web Senior Housing Directory is an online resource for locating and comparing housing options for Alzheimer's care, assisted living, and independent living. Users can search for housing by state, and request more information if desired. The site also provides articles and a glossary related to senior living.

California Advocates for Nursing Home Reform (CANHR)

650 Harrison Street, 2nd Floor

San Francisco, CA 94017

1-800-474-1116

www.canhr.org

Through direct advocacy, community education, legislation, and litigation, CANHR educates and supports long-term care consumers by judicially advocating regarding the rights and remedies under the law and creating a united voice for long-term care reform and humane alternatives to institutionalization.

Catholic Charities USA (CCUSA)

1731 King Street

Alexandria, VA 22314

703-549-1390

www.catholiccharitiesusa.org

CCUSA is a network of organizations offering nationwide services to older people, including counseling, homemaker and caregiver services, emergency assistance, group homes, and institutional care. CCUSA advocates for older people's Social Security benefits, employment opportunities, and housing. Publications describe Catholic Charities' programs for older people.

Catholic Golden Age (CGA)

National Headquarters
Olyphant, PA 18447
1-800-836-5699 (toll-free)
www.catholicgoldenage.org
CGA is the largest nonprofit organization for Catholics 50 and older. CGA sponsors charitable work that helps older people meet their social, physical, economic, intellectual, and spiritual needs. Contact CGA for various group insurance plans, discounts on eyeglasses, prescription drugs, and travel. Local CGA chapters provide activities for members, including disease prevention and health promotion programs.

Centers for Medicare and Medicaid Services (CMS)

7500 Security Boulevard
Baltimore, MD 21244
1-800-MEDICARE (633-4227) (toll-free) (Medicare hotline);
1-877-267-2323 (toll-free) (headquarters); 410-786-3000
www.cms..gov; www.medicare.gov
CMS, part of DHHS, administers health insurance through Medicare and Medicaid. CMS regulates hospitals, nursing homes, and home health agencies. Contact CMS for The Medicare Handbook and other publications on related topics.

Children of Aging Parents (CAPS)

P.O. Box 167
Richboro, PA 18954
1-800-227-7294 (toll-free)
www.caps4caregivers.org
CAPS is a nonprofit membership organization that provides information for family caregivers of older people. It serves as a clearinghouse for information on elder care resources, including a link to Medicare rights and coverage seminars. Links to support other groups and resources, plus an online newsletter are also available on the website.

Community Transportation Association of America (CTAA)

1341 G Street, NW, 10th Floor

Washington DC 20005

1-800-891-0590 (toll-free); 202-628-1480

www.ctaa.org

CTAA is a national association committed to removing barriers to isolation and improving mobility for all people. It offers educational programs and advocates making community transportation available, affordable, and accessible. CTAA provides information on transportation in medical emergencies and van conversions.

Delta Society

875 124th Avenue, NE, Suite 101

Bellevue, WA 98055

425-679-5500

www.deltasociety.org

The Delta Society is a national, nonprofit organization whose mission is improving human health through service and therapy animals. Its program, Pet Partners, brings volunteers and their pets to nursing homes, hospitals, and schools. The Society website has information and resources about the human-animal-health connection.

Department of Veterans Affairs (VA)

Washington DC 20420

1-800-827-1000 (toll-free)

www.va.gov

The VA, part of the Federal Government, provides benefits for eligible veterans and their families in outpatient clinics, medical centers, and nursing homes across the US. Contact the VA for information and publications on service locations and benefits, including comprehensive medical and dental care, other insurance benefits, vocational rehabilitation compensation, and pension.

Elder Care Online

Prism Innovations, Inc.,

50 Amuxen Court

Islip, NY 11751

www.ec-online.net

Elder Care Online offers information, education, and support for caregivers, safety advice, and links to additional caregiver resources on their website.

Eldercare Locator

National Association of Area Agencies on Aging

1730 Rhode Island Avenue, NW, Suite 1200

Washington DC 20036

1-800-677-1116 (toll-free)

www.eldercare.gov

The Eldercare Locator is a nationwide, directory assistance service helping older people and caregivers locate local support and resources for older Americans. It is funded by the Administration on Aging.

Elderweb

1305 Chadwick Drive

Normal, IL 61761

309-451-3319

www.elderweb.com

Elderweb is a research website for older people, professionals, and families seeking information on elder care and long-term care. Visit Elderweb for news and information on legal, financial, medical, and housing issues for older people and links to other websites.

Estate and Elder Planning Associates

70 Mitchell Boulevard, Suite 104

San Rafael, CA 94903

415-472-1396

www.haroldlustig.com

harold@haroldlustig.com

The mission of Estate and Elder Planning Associates is to help Baby-Boomers, seniors and their families achieve and maintain financial security through estate and long-term care planning, asset protection, and wealth transfer. The Estate and Elder Planning Associates works closely with elder law attorneys, geriatric care managers, VA and Medicaid/Medical specialists and qualified insurance brokers.

Family Caregiver Alliance

180 Montgomery Street, Suite 1100
San Francisco, CA 94104
1-800-445-8106 (toll-free), or 415-434-3388
www.caregiver.org
The Family Caregiver Alliance is a community-based nonprofit organization offering support services for those caring for adults with ADF, stroke, traumatic brain injuries, and other cognitive disorders. Programs and services include an information clearinghouse for publications, as well as a variety of online services.

Gray Panthers (GP)

1612 K Street, NW Suite 300
Washington, DC 20006
1-800-280-5362 (toll-free) 202-737-6637
www.graypanthers.org
Gray Panthers is a national advocacy organization of activists concentrating on social and economical issues. Local chapters organize intergenerational groups to address issues including universal health care, Medicare, preserving Social Security, affordable housing, and discrimination. Contact the national office for referrals to chapters, information on issues, links to resources for older people, and a list of publications.

Hill-Burton Free Care Program

Department of Health and Human Services
5600 Fishers Lane, Room 10-105
Rockville, MD 20857
1-800-638-0742 (toll-free)
www.hrsa.gov/hillburton
This site provides a list of hospitals and other health care facilities that receive federal funds for construction or modernization. In return, these facilities provide a specific amount of free or below-cost health care services to eligible people. Contact the program for a list of participating facilities as well as information on eligibility.

Legal Counsel for the Elderly (LCE)

American Association of Retired Persons (AARP)

Washington DC 20049

202-434-2120 or 1-888-OUR-AARP (687-2277) (toll-free)

www.aarp.org/lce

LCE, part of AARP, works to expand the availability of legal services to older people and to enhance the quality of those services. The National Volunteer Lawyers Project matches legal cases affecting large numbers of older people with volunteer law firms. The Senior Lawyers Project tests ways retired lawyers can provide free legal services to older people in need. The National Elderlaw Studies Program provides individual home study courses as well as a paralegal certificate from the Department of Agriculture Graduate School. Publications are available.

Lewy Body Dementia Association (LBDA)

PO Box 451429

Atlanta, GA 31145-9429

Caregiver Helpline: 800-539-9767

National Office: 404-935-6444

www.lbda.org

LBDA is a national nonprofit organization that provides information and support for individuals affected with Lewy body dementias, the second most common type of dementia after Alzheimer's disease, and their caregivers. Visit the website for educational resources, medical research updates, discussion forums, lists of local LBD support groups, and links to related organizations.

Meals on Wheels Association of America (MOWAA)

203 S. Union Street

Alexandria, VA 22314

703-548-5558

www.mowaa.org

MOWAA is a national, nonprofit organization providing training and grants to programs that provide food to older people. It also provides local program contact information for those who are frail, disabled, at-risk, or homebound.

MedicAlert Foundation

2323 Colorado Avenue

Turlock, CA 95382

1-888-633-4298 (toll-free) 209-668-3333 (outside the US)

www.medicalert.org

MedicAlert is a nonprofit, membership organization providing identification and medical information in emergencies. Contact MedicAlert for information about its membership services and costs.

Medicaid Practice Network (MPN)

c/o Elder Planning Law Center

www.eplawcenter.com

555 French Road, Suite 102

New Hartford, NY 13413

1-800-481-5290 (toll-free)

www.medicaidpracticenetwork.com

MPN is a national organization of lawyers who focus their practice on getting individuals qualified for Medicaid to pay nursing home costs in the shortest time possible, while protecting the maximum amount of assets. Each member attorney completes an extensive training program. MPN attorneys agree to provide free consultations to any individual concerned with long-term care and preserving their assets. Many are qualified to help find in-home care assistance and veteran benefits, to prevent nursing home placement. The website also provides a personal analysis tool showing whether one qualifies for certain exceptions while qualifying for benefits; for those who think they are ineligible because of their assets.

Medicare Rights Center (MRC)

1460 Broadway, 17th Floor

New York, NY 10036

212-869-3850

www.medicarerights.org

MRC is a national, nonprofit service helping older adults and people with disabilities get good, affordable health care. Available educational materials include a train-the-trainer manual, booklets on Medicare basics and Medicare home health.

National Alliance for Caregiving

4720 Montgomery Lane, 5th Floor

Bethesda, MD 20814

www.caregiving.org

The National Alliance for Caregiving is a nonprofit coalition focusing on issues of family caregiving. The Alliance offers information and publications for caregivers, and also supports the Family Care Resources Connection.

National Association for Home Care (NAHC)

228 7th Street, SE

Washington DC 20003

202-547-7424

www.nahc.org

NAHC is a trade association that promotes hospice and home care, sets standards of care, and conducts research on aging, health, and health care policy. Association publications include How to Choose a Home Care Provider and other free consumer guides on home care and hospice care.

National Association of Area Agencies on Aging (N4A)

1730 Rhode Island Avenue, NW Suite 1200

Washington DC 20036

1-800-677-1116 (toll-free) (Eldercare Locator) 202-872-0888

www.n4a.org

N4A is the umbrella organization for the AoA-funded Area Agencies on Aging. It also represents the interest of Title VI Native American aging programs. The Association administers the AoA-sponsored Eldercare Locator, a toll-free number linking older adults and their family members with local aging resources. N4A publishes the National Directory for Eldercare Information and Referral.

National Academy of Elder Law Attorneys (NAELA)

1577 Spring Hill Road, Suite 220

Vienna, VA 22182

703-942-5711

www.naela.org

The National Academy of Elder Law Attorneys, Inc. (NAELA) is a professional association of over 4,200 attorneys who are dedicated to improving the quality of legal services provided to seniors and people with special needs. NAELA members assist their clients with public benefits, probate and estate planning, guardianship/conservatorship, and health and long-term care planning, among other important issues.

National Association of States United for Aging & Disabilities (NASUAD)

1201 15th Street, NW, Suite 350

Washington DC 20005

202-898-2578

www.nasuad.org

NASUAD represents the nation's 56 officially designated state and territorial agencies on aging. The Center helps State and Area Agencies on Aging design, develop, and manage these care systems and develop state policies. A list of publications and materials on long-term and community-based care is available.

National Center for the Victims of Crime

2000 M Street NW, Suite 480

Washington DC 20036

Phone: 202-467-8700

INFOLINK: 1-800-394-2255 (toll-free)

www.ncvc.org

The National Center for the Victims of Crime website includes information for victims of any type of crime. The organization also has a help line, INFOLINK, which is intended to help callers find the most appropriate local services if they have been a victim of a crime.

National Center on Elder Abuse (NCEA)

www.ncea.aoa.gov

The NCEA, a division of the U.S. Administration on Aging (AoA) serves as a national resource center dedicated to the prevention of elder mistreatment. Their website contains a wealth of information on all aspects of elder abuse, including financial exploitation. It provides the ability to search for agencies and other resources on a state-by-state basis, as well as local telephone numbers for reporting elder abuse.

National Center on Senior Transportation

Telephone: 1-866-528-NCST (6278) (toll-free)

www.seniortransportation.net

The NCST offers extensive resources for transportation options for older adults. Based in Washington, D.C., the NCST is a partnership of Easter Seals Inc. and the National Association of Area Agencies on Aging. Staff from NCST answer questions about ADA rights and responsibilities, direct callers to additional resources, and help members of the aging services and transportation communities to address diverse accessibility issues.

National Committee to Preserve Social Security and Medicare (NCPSSM)

10 G Street, NE Suite 600

Washington DC 20004

1-800-966-1935 (toll-free) 202-216-0420

www.ncpssm.org

NCPSSM is a membership organization that works to protect and enhance federal programs vital to seniors' health and economic well-being via lobbyist efforts. It also provides information on seniors' rights, Medicare, Social Security, long-term care, and disability issues. Free information brochures are available.

National Committee for the Prevention of Elder Abuse (NCPEA)

1612 K Street, NW

Washington D.C. 20006

202-682-4140

www.preventelderabuse.org

The NCPEA's website has a designated section to help victims and those vulnerable to elder abuse. The site contains information on what to do if you feel someone you know is being abused, provides services available to stop abuse, and offers resources in the community.

National Consumers League's Fraud Center

www.fraud.org

The National Consumers League's Fraud Center allows individuals to submit an online complaint if they feel they have been a victim of possible fraud. The website includes information on common Internet and telemarketing fraud schemes and a specific section on "Scams Against Elderly," with tips for prevention.

The National Consumer Voice for Quality Long-Term Care

1828 L Street, NW Suite 801

Washington DC 20036-2211

202-332-2275

www.theconsumervoice.org

This organization advocates for nursing home reform, promotes quality standards, and works to empower residents. Contact The National Consumer Voice for information on community-based, consumer/citizen action, and long-term care ombudsmen groups. Publications on nursing homes and long-term care are available.

National Council on Aging (NCOA)

Washington DC 20024

1-800-424-9046 (toll-free) 202-479-1200

www.ncoa.org

The NCOA is a nonprofit service and advocacy organization whose mission is to improve the lives of older Americans. NCOA works with thousands of organizations across the country to help seniors find jobs and benefits, improve their health, live independently, and remain active in their communities; and also works with public agencies to improve policies.

National Elder Law Foundation (NELF)

6336 North Oracle Road, Suite 326

Tucson, AZ 85704

520-881-1076

www.nelf.com

NELF was founded in 1993 by the Board of Directors of the National Academy of Elder Law Attorneys, and has a membership of 392 Certified

Elder Law Attorneys (CELA) in 42 states and Washington, DC. Their website provides information on CELAs in member states.

National Family Caregivers Association (NFCA)
10400 Connecticut Avenue #500
Kensington, MD 20895-3944
1-800-896-3650 (toll-free) 301-942-6430
www.nfcacares.org
NFCA is a grassroots organization providing advocacy, support, and information for family members who care for chronically ill, older, or disabled relatives. There is no charge for family members to be on the mailing list and to receive the newsletter, Take Care! Contact NFCA for help finding resources.

National Hospice and Palliative Care Organization (NHPCO)
National Hospice Foundation (NHF)
1700 Diagonal Road, Suite 625
Alexandria, VA 22314
1-800-658-8898 (toll-free helpline)
www.nhpco.org
NHPCO is a nonprofit membership organization working to enhance the quality of life for individuals who are terminally ill and advocating for people in the final stage of life. In addition, the organization offers Caring Connections which provides resources and information to help people make decisions about end-of-life care and services, including care planning, caregiving, pain, financial issues, hospice, palliative care, grief, and loss. Publications, fact sheets, and website resources are available on topics including how to find and evaluate hospice services.

National Institute on Aging (NIA)
Bethesda, MD 20892-2292
1-800-222-2225 or 1-800-438-4380 (toll-free)
www.nia.nih.gov
NIA, part of NIH, conducts and supports biomedical, social, and behavioral research on aging processes, disease, and the special problems and needs of older people. NIA develops and disseminates publications on topics

such as the biology of aging, exercise, doctor/patient communication, and menopause. The Institute produces the Age Pages—a series of fact sheets for consumers on a wide range of subjects including nutrition, medications, forgetfulness, sleep, driving, and long-term care. Information, publications, referrals, resource lists, and database searches on Alzheimer's disease are available through the Institute-funded ADEAR Center.

National Rehabilitation Information Center (NARIC)

4200 Forbes Boulevard, Suite 202

Lanham, MD 20706

1-800-346-2742 (toll-free) 301-459-5900

www.naric.com

NARIC, funded by the Department of Education, provides information on rehabilitation of people with physical or mental disabilities. Contact NARIC for database searches on all types of physical and mental disabilities, as well as referrals to local and national facilities and organizations. All of NARIC's database information is available online for free.

National Senior Citizens Law Center (NSCLC)

1101 14th Street, NW Suite 400

Washington DC 20005

202-289-6976

www.nsclc.org

NSCLC offers consumers information, assistance to Legal Aid Offices, and private lawyers working on behalf of low-income older and disabled people. The Center does not accept individual clients, but acts as a clearinghouse of information on legal problems such as age discrimination, Social Security, pension plans, Medicaid, Medicare, nursing homes, and protective services.

National Senior Services Corps

1201 New York Avenue, NW

Washington DC 20525

202-606-5000; contact Senior Corps at 1-800-424-8867 (toll-free)

www.seniorcorps.org

The National Senior Services Corps is a network of federally-supported programs that help older people get involved in community service:

the Foster Grandparent Program (encouraging older people to work with children with special needs) and the Senior Companion Program (volunteers assisting older people with special needs in hospitals, social service agencies, or home health care agencies).

National Stroke Association (NSA)
9707 East Easter Lane, Building B
Centennial, CO 80112
1-800-STROKES (787-6537) (toll-free)
www.stroke.org
The Association provides information about stroke prevention, acute treatment, recovery, and rehabilitation to the public. NSA offers referrals to support groups, care centers, and local resources for stroke survivors, caregivers, and family members.

Older Women's League (OWL)
1828 L Street NW, Suite 801
Washington DC 20036
1-800-TAKE-OWL (825-3695) (toll-free) 703-812-7990
www.owl-national.org
OWL is a national organization advocating for the special concerns of older women. OWL helped develop the Campaign for Women's Health and the Women's Pension Policy Consortium. Contact OWL's 24-hour PowerLine for information about legal and political activity related to health care, access to housing, economic security, individual rights, and violence against women and older people. OWL newsletters are available.

Parkinson's Disease Foundation (PDF)
1359 Broadway, Suite 1509
New York, NY 10018
1-800-457-6676 (toll-free) 212-923-4700
www.pdf.org
PDF is a nonprofit organization providing research funding, information, and supportive services to people with Parkinson's disease. Contact the Foundation for referrals to specialists. Publications are available.

Pioneer Network

230 E. Ohio Street, Suite 400

Chicago, IL 60611

312-224-2574

www.pioneernetwork.net

Pioneer Network advocates for a radical culture change in eldercare, from long-term nursing home care to short-term transitional care to community-based care, to create homes in which elders thrive instead of merely survive. Pioneer Network's website provides information for providers in the form of research on their culture change model; and resource information to seniors and their families. The organization has built a national support network for over 30 state coalitions to advance culture change in their respective states.

SPRY Foundation

3916 Rosemary Street

Chevy Chase, MD 20815

301-656-3405

www.spry.org

SPRY—Setting Priorities for Retirement Years—is a nonprofit foundation that develops research and education programs to help older adults plan for a healthy and financially secure future. The website links consumers to national health resources.

Undertaken With Love: A Home Funeral Guide for Congregations and Communities

www.homefuneralmanual.org

Undertaken with Love is an online resource for information about family-directed, home-centered funeral planning. The site provides a home funeral manual, written in a study guide format, intended for congregational, hospice, or community groups. The guide may be downloaded at no cost, and a paperback version is also available for a minimal cost. The site also provides a blog, access to state home funeral laws, and additional resources.

Visiting Nurse Associations of America (VNAA)

900 19th Street, NW Suite 200

Washington DC 20006

202-384-1420

www.vnaa.org

VNAA is an association of nonprofit, community-based home health care providers. Visiting nurses offer quality in-home medical care including physical, speech, and occupational therapy, social services, and nutritional counseling. Local agencies operate adult day care centers, wellness clinics, hospices, and meals-on-wheels programs. A fact sheet and caregiver's handbook are available.

Volunteers of America

1660 Duke Street

Alexandria, VA 22314

1-800-899-0089 (toll-free) 703-341-5000

www.volunteersofamerica.org

Volunteers of America is a national, nonprofit, spiritually-based organization providing local human service programs and opportunities for individual community involvement. Specific programs include Aging With Options which provides information on housing, assisted living, meals-on-wheels, transportation, and health care services.

Well Spouse Foundation (WSF)

63 West Main Street, Suite H

Freehold, NJ 07728

1-800-838-0879 (toll-free) 732-577-8899

www.wellspouse.org

WSF is a not-for-profit association of spousal caregivers. It offers support to the wives, husbands, and partners of chronically ill or disabled people. The Foundation has a list of support groups nationwide and sponsors recreational respite opportunities.

GLOSSARY[57]

ACTIVITIES OF DAILY LIVING (ADLS). Routine actions such as eating, bathing, transferring (bed to chair), dressing, toileting, and continence. The inability to perform two or three of these activities is generally used to determine the level and kind of home health or nursing home care needed and to qualify for benefits under long-term care insurance.

ACUTE CARE. Immediate, short-term medical treatment for a serious illness or injury, usually in a hospital or skilled nursing facility. May be contrasted with chronic care.

ADULT DAY CARE. Care inside or outside the home provided for adults who require assistance with the activities of daily living or other largely non-medical supervision. Possibly includes minimal medical-related services such as supervising medicine-taking. Often includes social and recreational programs and, sometimes, occupational and physical therapy. Primarily intended for care during the hours that family members or other informal caregivers are at work, rather than care on a 24-hour basis.

ADULT DAY CARE FACILITIES. Community-based centers that provide comprehensive services ranging from health assessment and care to social programs for older persons who need some supervision. They may be operated by hospitals, nursing homes, local governments, or private groups. Out-of-pocket costs vary. Medicare does not cover adult day care.

ALTERNATE CARE. A plan mutually agreeable to you, the insurance company of your long-term care policy, and those individuals preparing the plan. The alternate care you receive can include special treatment at home or in other facilities. Benefit levels may differ from your usual coverage. Definitions used in insurance policies may vary from policy to policy. Insurers may use this term to extend coverage to care in facilities of the future not yet identified or in use.

---

57 Reprinted with permission from American Independent Marketing website, 2010.

ALZHEIMER'S DISEASE. A progressive and irreversible organic disease, typically occurring in the elderly and characterized by degeneration of the brain cells, leading to dementia, of which Alzheimer's is the single most common cause. Progresses from forgetfulness to severe memory loss and disorientation, lack of concentration, loss of ability to calculate numbers, and finally to increased severity of all symptoms and significant personality changes.

ASSISTED LIVING FACILITY. A non-specific term referring to any setting that provides living arrangements and assistance for the elderly and/ or disabled. Also called Adult Foster Care.

BED RESERVATION BENEFIT. In some long-term care policies, a benefit paid to maintain the insured's space in a nursing home facility when the insured must be hospitalized temporarily.

BENEFIT AMOUNT OR LIMITS. In general, the maximum amount payable by an insurer to an insured person for the specific benefits contracted under an insurance policy. In long-term care insurance, generally refers to the daily benefit amount for which the insured has contracted and which is payable for each day of long-term care the insured receives in accordance with the policy's provisions.

BENEFIT CAP. The lifetime dollar limitation of a long-term care policy.

BENEFIT MAXIMUM. Either a certain number of days or a dollar amount expressing what a policy will pay for a given service. This is the "most" that the policy will pay. It may pay less due to other policy limitations.

BENEFIT PERIOD. In a long-term care insurance policy, the maximum length of time specified in the contract during which benefits will be paid. Periods available vary considerably from policy to policy and insurer to insurer, ranging from as short as one year to as long as a lifetime. In some cases, especially for longer benefit periods, a maximum dollar limit may also apply. For example, the policy might provide for a lifetime benefit period capped at $500,000 maximum benefits. When $500,000 in benefits has been paid, benefits cease even if the insured is still living and receiving long-term care.

BENEFIT PERIOD (MEDICARE). Also called "Spell of Illness." A period of time that begins on or with the first day of confinement in either a hospital or nursing home and ends at a specific point. As an example, Medicare's first 60 days of hospitalization begins on the first day admitted to the hospital and ends when the beneficiary has gone 60 days without being re-admitted to the facility.

CARE COORDINATION BENEFIT. A benefit in newer long-term care policies that pays consultation fees for a professional, such as a registered visiting nurse or a medical social worker, to periodically assess and make recommendations about the insured's care program. For example, consultation might begin at a specified time after the insured has been confined to a skilled nursing facility. The purpose is to adjust services when and if the individual's care needs change. Also called personal care advisor or personal care advocate benefit.

CAREGIVER. A non-specific term describing either a skilled or non-skilled person who provides some type of care for another. In long-term care policies, types of care and types of caregivers are generally defined for purposes of identifying covered services.

CASE MANAGEMENT. A professional service which arranges and coordinates health and/or social services through assessment, service plan development, modification, monitoring, and quality assurance.

CHRONIC CARE. Continuous, long-term care for persons suffering from chronic conditions. May be contrasted with acute care.

COGNITIVE IMPAIRMENT. A defect in or loss of all or part of an individual's memory, judgment, perception, reasoning, or other intellectual functioning as medically diagnosed. Often one of the triggers for benefit payments under a long-term care insurance policy.

COGNITIVE IMPAIRMENT REINSTATEMENT PROVISION. A provision in some long-term care policies that allows a policy that has lapsed because the insured did not pay the premium to be reinstated for full benefits if the premiums are paid within six months after the lapse. Typically, the insured's physician must certify that the insured suffered a cognitive impairment that presumably caused the individual to fail to pay the premium on time.

COINSURANCE. A cost-sharing requirement which provides that a Medicare beneficiary must assume a portion or percentage of the costs of covered services. Medicare coinsurance amounts are usually stated either in dollars or as a percentage of the reasonable charge for services.

CONTINUING CARE RETIREMENT COMMUNITY (CCRC).

A combination of residential and nursing home facilities that might also include a broad variety of recreational, social, medical, and other services. Requires a significant entrance fee followed by monthly payments to retain residency and services. As one option for obtaining and paying for long-term care, CCRCs are currently considered affordable for fewer than 10 percent of retirees. Also called life care community.

CONVALESCENT CARE. Another term often used for short-term custodial care and refers to a "recovery" period after an illness or injury when some assistance may be needed that does not require skilled care.

CO-PAYMENT. Used interchangeably with coinsurance. Co-payment is usually a set dollar amount rather than a percentage.

CUSTODIAL CARE. In the context of long-term care or Medicare, refers to assistance requiring the lowest level of skills, helping with activities of daily living, but not with medical care. Can be provided by people who have no medical training, sometimes by aides trained in caregiving skills and frequently provided informally by family members or other unpaid volunteers. Custodial care services, which may be performed in a nursing home, the individual's home, or some other setting, are the most common type of services required by the elderly and the disabled.

CUSTODIAL CARE FACILITY. A care facility providing the lowest skill level of care, primarily assistance with activities of daily living and minimal skilled nursing care, the latter usually limited to supervision of medicine-taking.

CUSTODIAL NURSING CARE. Also called **Maintenance Nursing Care** or simply Maintenance Care; it is care which is primarily done for the purpose of meeting an individual's daily personal needs such as bathing, eating, or taking medications. It may be provided by persons without special training or skills. If given in a hospital or nursing home, the care will usually be under the direction of a doctor. Also called custodial care.

DAILY BENEFIT AMOUNT. In a long-term care policy the specific amount of insurance the policy pays for each covered day of long-term care as defined in the policy. The insured may choose from a wide range of daily benefit amounts and, under some policies, different amounts for different types of care, such as a higher daily benefit for nursing home care and a somewhat lower benefit for home care. Options available vary widely among insurers and policies.

DEATH BENEFIT. In some long-term care policies, a benefit payable to the insured's survivors or estate if the insured dies before a specified age, often 65 or 70. The benefit amount is a refund of premiums the insured paid, minus the amount of any benefits the insured received while living.

DEDUCTIBLE. The amount of health care expense that a Medicare beneficiary must first incur and pay out-of-pocket annually before Medicare will begin payment for covered services. Medicare deductibles include the Part A hospital deductible, the Part B deductible for all covered services under Part B, and the blood deductible.

DEMENTIA. Deterioration of mental ability, generally caused by organic brain disease, less often by psychological factors. Characterized by disorientation and loss of memory and intellect, also called **organic dementia.**

DIAGNOSTIC RELATED GROUP (DRG). A classification based upon an individual's medical diagnosis at the time the individual is admitted to a hospital for treatment that is funded by Medicare and determines in advance how much Medicare will reimburse the hospital for treatment regardless of the length of the hospital stay. The DRG classification is part of Medicare's Prospective Payment System (PPS), designed to help contain costs. This has resulted in shorter hospital stays and an increase in nursing home admissions since its implementation in 1984. Also called **Diagnosis Related Groups.**

ELIMINATION PERIOD. In insurance policies, a period after the onset of an illness or injury during which no benefits are paid, effectively providing for a deductible. Common in long-term care policies, although some insurers offer policies with no elimination period. Sometimes called a waiting period, which is technically incorrect from the viewpoint of the insurance industry, in which a waiting period is a different phenomenon.

EMPLOYER-SPONSORED LTC INSURANCE. Long-term care insurance made available by an employer to its employees, similar to other types of group insurance. Many employer-sponsored LTC plans may also be offered to employee family members including spouses, parents, and parents of spouses and children, depending on the particular plan and the insurer.

EXCESS CHARGE. Also called **Balance Billing,** it relates to Medicare Part B charges. It is the amount of the medical bill which is above the dollar figure allowed by Medicare.

EXCLUSION. A condition not covered under a health insurance or long-term care insurance policy.

EXPLANATION OF MEDICARE BENEFITS (EOMB OR EOB). The statement of payment from Medicare; it shows the amount charged by the medical provider, the amount approved by Medicare, and the amount actually paid by Medicare. It is this statement that is submitted to the insurance company for payment under the Medigap policy.

EXTENDED CARE FACILITY. An institutionalized setting outside of a hospital that provides 24-hour skilled nursing care as prescribed by a physician.

FREE LOOK PROVISION. An insurance policy provision required by most states, allowing the policy owner to inspect the policy for a specified period of time, often 10, 15, 20, or 30 days and to return the policy to the insurer, if desired, for a refund of the entire premium.

FRAUD. The outright misrepresentation of facts with the direct intent to defraud either Medicare and/or an insurance company.

GATEKEEPERS. In long-term care insurance, refers to policy provisions, restrictions, or limitations that qualify the insured to begin receiving benefits, such as being referred for care by a physician, being unable to perform a specified number of activities of daily living, having a prior hospital confinement, or others. Technically, these are the coverage triggers in long-term care policies. Also called **safety nets**.

GUARANTEED RENEWABLE POLICY. A policy that guarantees the insured may renew the policy up to a specified age, or for life, as long as the insured pays the premiums. The insurance company may increase the premiums on guaranteed renewable policies for all policies of that particular type, but may not increase the premium for any individual policy.

HEALTH INSURANCE CLAIM NUMBER. The number listed on the beneficiary's Medicare card; it will consist of nine digits followed by one or more letters. The nine digits represent the Social Security number of either the beneficiary or their spouse, depending upon whose income it is based upon.

HEALTH MAINTENANCE ORGANIZATION (HMO). A type of service provider that arranges for both health care services and payment for those services. Requires members to pay a pre-set monthly fee covering a broad range of services rather than payment for individual services. Members must use medical practitioners and facilities approved by the HMO, usually at a location the HMO owns and operates, and using medical personnel employed by the HMO. HMOs may contract with Medicare to offer Medicare beneficiaries all services covered by fee-for-service Medicare. When a Medicare beneficiary joins an HMO, he or she must usually "sign over" their Medicare benefits to that HMO.

HOME HEALTH CARE. A type of medical care that is gaining popularity as people attempt to stay out of nursing homes. It is growing rapidly as technology provides equipment that is more portable and personnel receive additional training. As the name implies, services are performed at an individual's home, as opposed to an outside facility. Generally may refer to any level of care and a wide range of skilled and non-skilled services, including part-time nursing care, various types of therapy, assistance with activities of daily living, and homemaker services such as cleaning and meal preparation. For Medicare purposes, this term refers specifically to intermittent, physician-ordered medical services or treatment and should not be confused with definitions contained in long-term care policies.

HOME HEALTH CARE AGENCY. Either a private commercial venture or a state-operated organization that is licensed to provide health care and/or homemaker services to individuals who need assistance but need not be institutionalized. Those who actually provide the services are commonly referred to as home health aides who may or may not have to be specifically trained and licensed or certified in particular states. Newer long-term care policies often pay for such services performed in an insured person's home.

HOMEMAKER SERVICES. A variety of non-skilled at-home services, including shopping, meal preparation, laundry services, housekeeping, and similar activities provided either by employees of private home health agencies or state agencies. Some long-term care policies pay a benefit for such services.

HOSPICE. An organization which primarily provides pain relief, symptom management, and support services for terminally ill patients and their families.

HOSPICE CARE. Care for the terminally ill. Includes some medical assistance primarily for pain control and making the ill person comfortable, as well as counseling services for the ill and their families. May occur at home or in an institutionalized setting. Medicare provides benefits under Part A for this type of care; there are restrictions and qualifications that apply.

HOSPITAL INSURANCE (PART A). That part of the Medicare program which helps pay for inpatient hospital care, inpatient care in a skilled nursing facility, home health care, and hospice care.

INFLATION PROTECTION. An option offered on some long-term care policies which can increase the maximum daily and lifetime benefits to combat inflation. The protection is generally five percent per year, but varies from policy to policy as to whether the increase is calculated at simple or compound interest.

INTERMEDIATE CARE. In the context of long-term care and Medicare, refers to a level of nursing services performed intermittently, rather than around the clock, by professional medical personnel, usually a registered or licensed practical nurse or other medical practitioners such as licensed therapists.

INTERMEDIATE CARE FACILITY (ICF). A care facility providing skilled nursing care on an as-needed basis rather than on a 24-hour basis, as well as custodial care associated with the intermediate level care. An Intermediate Facility may not provide Skilled Care and, therefore, may not be certified by Medicare, since that is the only level of care which they will pay for.

LEVELS OF CARE can include these three levels of long-term care:

Skilled Care. 24-hour-a-day prescribed care provided by licensed medical professionals who are under the direct supervision of a physician.

Intermediate Care. Prescribed care that can be provided on an intermittent, rather than continuous basis—for example, physical therapy.

Custodial Care. Care that assists people with daily living requirements, such as dressing, eating, and personal hygiene.

LIFETIME MAXIMUM. A set benefit amount payable under a contract or policy. In some types of contracts, benefits that have been used are renewable, but usually only up to a specific figure. That specific figure is the lifetime maximum. It is the total amount of benefits payable during the lifetime of the policy.

LIFETIME RESERVE DAYS. Hospitalization (Part A) under Medicare from the 91st through 150th day of confinement. This period of consecutive hospitalization is not renewable; once used, the benefit is gone.

LIMITING CHARGE. Also called Limiting Physician Charge. This refers to the COBRA 1989 and 1990 legislation which, among other things, attempts to put a cap or ceiling on the amount medical providers charge for their services under Part B of Medicare.

LONG-TERM CARE (LTC). A wide range of medical and non-medical services ranging from custodial help with activities of daily living to occasional nursing care to skilled nursing services provided to people who are physically or mentally unable to provide independent care for themselves. Usually used to describe care for the elderly, although younger disabled persons also utilize long-term care services. Care may be needed while recovering from an accident or illness, during an extended period of disability, or simply as a result of the normal aging process. Home health care, adult day care, respite care, and nursing home stays fall into the category of long-term care.

LONG-TERM CARE (LTC) INSURANCE. Insurance that covers expenses incurred when the insured receives specified services associated with extended care in a variety of settings, including the individual's home, nursing homes, and community-based facilities such as assisted living facilities and adult day care centers.

LONG-TERM CARE RIDER. An attachment that may be added to some life insurance and other types of insurance policies to allow some or all of the death benefit or other primary benefit to be used to help pay for long-term care costs under situations defined in the policy.

MAINTENANCE NURSING CARE. Also called simply **Maintenance Care** or **Custodial Care**; it is care which is primarily done for the purpose of meeting an individual's personal needs (activities of daily living) such as bathing, eating, dressing, or taking medications. It may be provided by persons without professional training or skills. Even so, this type of care is usually given under a doctor's orders.

MAXIMUM. A limit on the amount that a plan will pay. It may be expressed as a dollar amount or as a time limit.

MAXIMUM DAILY BENEFIT. The amount designated in a long-term care policy up to which it will pay benefits per day for nursing home care. It also determines the amount per visit payable for home health care.

MEDICAID. A joint federal-state welfare program that pays for medical care for those with very low incomes. It will cover nursing home costs and some very limited home health care but only after most assets and income have been exhausted. Being on Medicaid may reduce or limit the choice of nursing homes. Called Medi-Cal in California.

MEDICAL INSURANCE (PART B). That part of Medicare which helps pay for medically necessary physicians' services, outpatient hospital services, home health care services, and a number of other medical services and supplies that are not covered by Medicare Part A. Part B is also called

MEDICARE. The federal government-sponsored health care program funded and operated by the Social Security Administration, providing medical benefits for individuals over the age of 65, some disabled persons, and those with end-stage renal disease. Automatically includes Part A Hospital Insurance. Part B Supplementary Medical Insurance covers physicians' services and other outpatient care and is optionally available for a monthly charge. There are some co-payments and deductibles on both Parts A and B. The dollar amounts of these may change each year (check with your local Social Security office for current details). Medicare does not provide benefits for custodial or intermediate nursing home care, or long-term care.

MEDICARE SUPPLEMENT INSURANCE. Private insurance policies that "supplement" the benefits provided by Medicare. A Medicare supplement policy is sometimes called a "Medigap" policy supplement because it fills in the "gaps" left by Medicare benefits. Generally speaking, Medicare supplements will pay only if Medicare approves some portion of the services provided. The general rule of thumb is: Medicare supplements supplement Medicare. Therefore, if Medicare totally denies the claim, the supplement policy will deny the claim also. Medicare supplements do not provide long-term care benefits.

MODEL POLICY (NAIC). Any insurance policy prototype, including a long-term care policy, developed and recommended by the National Association of Insurance Commissioners (NAIC) and offered to insurance companies and to the individual states as a minimum standard for approval purposes. Neither insurers nor states are required to accept or adopt NAIC models, although many do. NAIC's model long-term care policy is more liberal than the first generation of private LTC policies, but less liberal than many private LTC policies currently available.

NATIONAL ASSOCIATION OF INSURANCE COMMISSIONERS (NAIC). An organization of insurance commissioners and superintendents that promotes communication about insurance regulation and practices and recommends model laws related to insurance in all states for the purpose of helping standardize laws and practices, and promoting consumer protection.

NONFORFEITURE FEATURE. A provision in some long-term care policies offering a guarantee that certain policy benefits will remain available even if the insured stops paying premiums. One type of nonforfeiture is a paid-up policy providing the same benefits for a shorter period or lower benefits for the same period as the original policy. Return of premium benefits are another form of nonforfeiture.

NURSING HOME. A non-specific term that refers to any of several types of facilities designed to provide one or more levels of care for persons who need assistance. May include skilled, intermediate, and/or custodial care facilities.

NURSING HOME CARE. Care provided in a skilled nursing facility where all three levels of care (skilled, intermediate, and custodial) are provided. In order to be licensed, nursing homes must meet appropriate standards for the state in which they operate. They may or may not be Medicare-approved.

ORGANIC DISORDER. An alteration in the structure of an organ caused by disease as opposed to psychosomatic or functional disorders in which no evidence of organic problems exist even though some impairment exists. In long-term care policies, often referred to as demonstrable organic disease and should specifically include Alzheimer's and Parkinson's diseases, both of which have organic origins. Other associated terms are dementia and organic dementia.

PAID-UP POLICY. In long-term care insurance, it is generally the operation of a nonforfeiture feature under which the insured's coverage continues for some period based on the amount of premiums paid when the policy lapses. Methods for providing the paid-up policy may include full benefits for a shorter benefit period or partial benefits for the full original benefit period. Some policies also have a provision which pays up the policy under specified conditions upon the death of an insured spouse. Some companies offer limited or single payment premium modes that result in paid-up policies when a specified number of annual premiums have been paid.

PARKINSON'S DISEASE. An organic brain disease caused by degeneration of or damage to the basal nerve cells of the brain, usually in elderly people and is characterized by tremors, muscle rigidity, and a shuffling walk. About a third of diagnosed patients progress to dementia after 10 or more years if untreated. Symptoms are less severe with drug treatment. It is often covered by name in newer policies.

MEDICARE PART A. That part of Medicare that covers inpatient hospital care, skilled nursing facility care, home health care, and hospice care. Also called Part A Hospital Insurance.

MEDICARE PART B. That part of Medicare that covers physicians' services, the cost of medical equipment and supplies, outpatient hospital services, and a variety of other medical services not covered by Medicare Part A. Also called Part B Medical Insurance.

PARTICIPATING MEDICAL PROVIDER. A Participating Physician is one who accepts the portion of the bill that Medicare approves as payment for his or her services. Medicare will then pay 80 percent of that amount approved and either the patient or their insurance company must pay the 20 percent remaining.

PARTNERSHIP FOR LONG-TERM CARE INSURANCE.
Arrangements between some states and certain private insurance companies to provide long-term care insurance. Subject to the specific legal requirements for each state, these partnerships help protect the assets of insured persons who typically must become nearly impoverished before qualifying for Medicaid (Medi-Cal in California) assistance for long-term care costs. In general, the state approves the long-term care policies offered by insurers who agree to include state-mandated provisions. Insured persons who purchase the approved policies may protect one dollar in assets for every one dollar in benefits paid by the private insurance coverage. The purpose of these plans is to shift some of the burden for long-term care from Medicaid programs to private insurance while at the same time allowing insurance purchasers to keep assets they would otherwise have to spend in order to qualify for Medicaid when the private insurance benefits are exhausted.

PEER REVIEW ORGANIZATION (PRO).
A group of practicing doctors and other health care professionals under contract to the federal government to review the care provided to Medicare patients. Also known as a Quality Review Organization (QRO).

PERSONAL CARE ADVISOR.
A benefit offered by some long-term care policies. Also called Care Coordination Benefit.

PRE-EXISTING CONDITION.
Health conditions diagnosed or treated prior to the effective date of a health care or long-term care policy.

Precise definitions differ widely among health insurers and policy types. Policies vary in whether or not they exclude coverage for these conditions and, if so, for how long.

POLICY FORM NUMBER.
Legal designation used by an insurance company when filing a specific policy form with the state insurance department.

POLICY SUMMARY. A summation of selected features of an insurance policy prepared and attached to the policy by the insurer for delivery to the policy owner/insured person.

PRIMARY CARE PHYSICIAN. Generally refers to HMOs or other types of member organizations; the doctor selected by the enrollee is called the Primary Care Physician since that doctor is in charge of managing that member's health care needs.

PRIMARY CARE SERVICES. Under Medicare, they are designated to include consultation services, hospital in-patient services, and psychiatric services. These services are often referred to as "Evaluation and Management Services."

PROSPECTIVE PAYMENT SYSTEM (PPS). Federally mandated method intended to control Medicare costs under which Medicare pays a fixed reimbursement to hospitals based on the individual's diagnosis rather than on the actual cost of treatment. Costs are determined in advance—prospectively—rather than after the fact or retrospectively. Implemented by classifying patients into diagnostic related groups (DRGs) that dictate the amount Medicare pays for treatment.

REGISTERED NURSE (RN). An individual who provides nursing services after completing a course of study that results in a baccalaureate degree and who has been legally authorized or registered to practice as an RN and use the RN designation after passing examination by a state board of nurse examiners or similar state authority.

REHABILITATIVE (RESTORATIVE) CARE. Skilled care provided by a trained medical person (physical therapist, RN, speech therapist). Its purpose is to restore health following an accident, injury, or illness. Medicare pays for a limited amount of this type of care.

REINSTATED BENEFITS. When a policy has lapsed due to nonpayment of premiums, benefits may be reinstated at the company's option. It is common for the company to determine proof of insurability before it will do so.

RENEWABLE AT THE OPTION OF THE INSURANCE COMPANY. This refers to policy contract renewability. The insurance company can choose to cancel the policy on an individual basis.

RESPITE CARE. A few hours to several days of assistance to give a temporary rest or break from caregiving for the individual's usual caretaker, often a family member or friend. The service can be provided at home or in a facility setting such as a nursing home. Benefits for respite care are included in most long-term care insurance policies. Medicare covers respite care only for the terminally ill under their hospice program.

Restoration of Benefits means once you are benefit-free (as defined in your particular policy) for a specified length of time, usually six months, those benefits already paid out are restored. Not all long-term care policies offer this benefit.

RETURN OF PREMIUM BENEFIT. A type of nonforfeiture benefit included in some long-term care policies that provides a cash value accumulation and return of premiums in the future to insured persons who receive no policy benefits or minimal benefits while the policy is in force. Exact provisions vary from policy to policy, but generally provide a greater return the longer the policy is in force and usually deduct the amount of any claims paid before returning premiums to the insured.

RIDER. An attachment to an insurance policy that changes or adds provisions not included in the original policy. There is an additional charge for riders added at the insured's option to provide additional benefits for the insured. Also called an **endorsement.**

SAFETY NETS. SEE GATEKEEPERS.

SENILE DEMENTIA. Outdated term referring to organic dementia associated with old age. Dementia was formerly divided by age of onset into senile (over age 65) and pre-senile (under age 65). But this division is now considered artificial since symptoms are identical regardless of age.

SKILLED NURSING CARE. In the context of long-term care or Medicare, refers to the highest level of professional medical care, characterized by 24-hour supervision by a registered or licensed practical nurse as ordered by a physician. For Medicare, must be performed in a skilled nursing facility as specifically defined by Medicare, a requirement that may or may not apply under a long-term care policy depending on the insurer.

SKILLED NURSING FACILITY (SNF). A facility licensed by the individual state, and one that may be certified by Medicare, providing care that requires the highest level of medical skills with continuous, 24-hour attention from a registered or licensed practical nurse, under a physician's orders and/or supervision. May also provide Intermediate or Custodial Care and makes care available from other medical practitioners and for emergency services.

SPOUSAL DISCOUNT. A premium reduction, usually from 10 to 25 percent of the premium, which some insurers provide when both a wife and husband purchase long-term care policies. Insurers offering such discounts sometimes do so for two people who permanently reside together whether or not they are spouses.

THERAPEUTIC DEVICES. May include hospital beds, crutches, wheelchairs, ramps, intravenous pumps, and respirators.

UNDERWRITING. The process of examining and investigating an applicant for insurance to determine whether or not the insurance company is willing to provide insurance coverage and on what basis.

WAITING PERIOD. In some health insurance policies, a period during which no benefits are paid immediately after the policy goes into effect. Sometimes used incorrectly as a synonym for an insurance policy's elimination period.

WAIVER OF PREMIUM PROVISION. Any provision included within or as a rider to an insurance policy providing that, when specified conditions exist, the policy will continue in force without further premium payment. When the specified conditions no longer exist, the insured person resumes paying premiums.

ABOUT
HAROLD LUSTIG, CLU, ChFC

Harold is President of Estate and Elder Planning Associates and the Managing Member of Lustig Financial Services, LLC. He has been an insurance and financial advisor and long-term care planning specialist for more than 32 years. Harold has been primarily focusing on the needs of seniors and their families for the last 12 years. Harold helps people with such issues as wealth preservation, asset management, increasing income while reducing taxes, estate planning, and how to pay for long-term care without going broke.

Harold has been quoted in the *Boston Globe, Mercury News*, and the old *San Francisco Examiner*. His articles have been in the Investment Advisor, the Accountant, and the Society of Certified Senior Advisors, and he has been a syndicated columnist for Patch.com. He has spoken nationally for the Financial Planning Association Advanced Estate Planning Retreats in Houston and Tampa as well as at several FPA Regional Conferences in San Francisco. Harold is a member of the National Speakers Association. .

Harold also wrote the first financial and estate planning book for lesbian and gay couples which was published in 1999 by Random House and titled *4 Steps to Financial Security for Lesbian and Gay Couples*.

Harold is a Chartered Life Underwriter (CLU) and a Chartered Financial Consultant (ChFC). He is an Investment Advisor Representative with Lustig Financial Services, LLC, registered in the State of California as an Investment Advisor. Harold is licensed to sell life and health insurance, annuities, as well as provide advisory services.

Harold and his wife, Clarinda Cole Lustig live with their two cats, Oscar Himit and Jewel, in Greenbrae, CA. Clarinda, an RN, works with seniors in need of long term-care as a Geriatric Care Manager.

INDEX

D

E

F

G

H

I

L

M

N

O

P

Q

R

S

T

U

Z